The Book of Herbal Teas

A Guide to Gathering, Brewing, and Drinking

BY SARA PERRY

Photography by Christopher Irion

CHRONICLE BOOKS

SAN FRANCISCO

Printed in Hong Kong.

Book and cover design: Ursula Brookbank

Library of Congress Cataloging-in-Publication Data:
    Perry, Sara.
    The book of herbal teas: a guide to gathering, brew-
    ing, and drinking / Sara Perry; photographs by
    Christopher Irion
    120 p.   17.5 x 20.4 cm.
    Includes bibliographical references and index.
    ISBN 0-8118-1337-1
    1. Herbal Teas. 2. Herbs. I. Title.
    TX415.P48 1996
    641.6'372—dc20   96-1605
                        CIP

Distributed in Canada by Raincoast Books,
8680 Cambie Street, Vancouver, B.C. V6P 6M9

10 9 8 7 6 5 4 3 2 1

Chronicle Books
85 Second Street
San Francisco, CA 94105

TO MY FATHER,
Elmer Wheaton, who not only taught me to
recognize every plant we'd see while riding
Sierra and Chico along the trails of
Mandeville Canyon, but to appreciate their
individual beauty; to my mother, Martha
Wheaton, whose love of gardening I remember
every time I tend my own garden; and to
Bette Sinclair, a dear friend, who is always
there to help, encourage, support, and toast
all of life's unpredictable treasures.

Acknowledgments

I WOULD LIKE TO THANK my friends and colleagues who shared their time, ideas, good thoughts, and herbal pleasures, especially Patty Merrill at Powell's Books for Cooks in Portland, Oregon; herbalist and educator Judy Siegel; Juanita Crampton at Sattwa; Will Simonds at the Berry Botanic Garden in Portland, Oregon; Patti Chambers; Colby Whipple and all the Portland Art Museum's After Hours gang; tea master Steven Smith; and best of all, my husband, Pete Perry. Thanks also go to Catherine Glass, my editor and friend, whose encouragement, wisdom, and attention to detail are very much appreciated and valued.

Special thanks go to Leslie Jonath at Chronicle Books, who takes the time to smooth an author's way; to Sarah Putman and Laura Lovett, who provided inexhaustible and expert support. And always, my thanks go to Bill LeBlond, senior editor at Chronicle Books, for his support and friendship. I'm truly blessed.

—Sara Perry

TO SUSAN ESLICK, my most useful critic, for all her help. To my mother, Ruth Irion, and sister, Lenore Irion, for invaluable help with props. Also to Jim and Karen Shay, Catherine Gailloud, Carolyn Hubinger of Tisane, and the greengrocers and herbalists of Rainbow Grocery.

—Christopher Irion

Contents

Introduction

WHENEVER I WENT CAMPING with my dad, we always found unexpected treasures. When I was eight, we went on an overnight in the San Gabriel Mountains near Los Angeles. The fire was laid, the sleeping bags were stretched out on a mat of summer grasses, and it was getting chilly. Dad reached beside me on the ground where we were resting and began collecting a handful of tiny, daisy-like flowers. He dropped them in our tin cups and poured in some boiling water. I couldn't figure out what he was doing. Until I tasted it. Magic, I thought. In a way, I was right. My first cup of chamomile tea with my dad left me amazed that the world around us offered such hidden gifts. (The tea also left me relaxed and sleepy.) ❧Herbal teas have always held magic and mystery in a cup. No other beverage has such a place in the heart and culture of every civilization. Herbal teas can create visions, cure ailments, and make a simply delicious beverage. ❧If you think herbs add variety to your pestos, pastas, and potpourris, come see what their distinctive flavors can do to water. Discover the difference between herbal tea and the "other" tea and find out how herbs can affect your well-being. Learn how to prepare the perfect cup of hot or iced tea and how to create your own sublime beverages with a single herb, herbal blends, exotic spices, and fresh-squeezed juices. If you are interested in growing or gathering your own herbs, here are hints and how-tos, from cultivating urban spaces to fine-tuning your supermarket savvy. You'll also find an herbal guide that describes the essential characteristics of forty popular tea herbs and what you need to know to grow, harvest, brew, and enjoy them. Welcome to the tantalizing world of herbal tea.

At the Beginning

TODAY, WHEN YOU ORDER a cup of tea in a restaurant, the first question you're likely to hear is, "Do you want regular or herbal?" Is there a difference? Broadly speaking, all teas are herbal. The classic definition of an herb is any plant that has a fleshy stem—unlike the woody tissue of shrubs and trees—and dies back at the end of its growing season. In the world of herbal teas, an herb is any plant, shrub, or tree capable of affecting our lives through its aroma, taste, flavor, or therapeutic use. Every part of the plant is considered appropriate, from its leaves to its stems, berries, seeds, flowers, roots, and bark. For centuries, beverage connoisseurs considered tea to be the specific brew of one plant, a camellia-like bush with the Latin name *Thea sinensis*. When its fresh leaves are plucked, they're processed in one of three ways, resulting in three different kinds of tea: green, black, or oolong. When a beverage is made from infusing these leaves in boiling water, it's referred to as traditional, true, or China tea. In this book, we refer to it as China tea.

The histories of herbal tea and of herbal medicine are often intertwined and difficult to separate. In China over three thousand years ago, Emperor Shen Nung discovered a leaf floating in his bowl of steaming spring water. Finding the beverage far more refreshing than plain water, this patriarch of herbal medicine began trying other leaves and wrote down his observations in *Pen Tsao Ching,* the first known herbal. According to legend, the emperor had a transparent abdomen and so could easily observe the effects of several hundred herbs and waters on his internal organs.

In India, herbs have always been a part of religious and everyday life. According to Hindu myth, the gods instructed human physicians in the *Ayurveda,* or the Way of Life, and even before the written word, these medical doctrines were passed down through oral teachings. The most famous text was the *Charaka Samhita,* which mentioned the use of at least five hundred herbs. While many of these potent beverages had curative powers, the ancient Hindus also created pleasant herbal drinks for inner peace and harmony.

Aromatic herbs were used to honor gods, cure the sick, and embalm the dead in ancient Egypt. The *Ebers Papyrus,* a remarkable document dating to 1550 B.C., lists such familiar curative herbs as cardamom, fennel, thyme, and anise, which were used in cooking, beverages, aromatic oils, and cosmetics.

In turn, the ancient Greeks and Romans built upon earlier herbal knowledge and added to it. The Greeks were scholars who studied, tested, and categorized the effects of herbs, and their writings became the basis of herbal medicine throughout medieval Europe. Hippocrates (468–377 B.C.) not only initiated the practices of modern medicine but taught the value of herbs in curing diseases *and* the dangers of poisonous hemlock. In A.D. 60, the Greek physician Dioscorides wrote *De Mateira Medica,* which became the standard by which all other herbals were judged for fifteen hundred years. Many of the over five hundred herbal uses he recorded—

such as using parsley as a diuretic—are still used with effect today.

The Romans were great travelers. Conquering most of Europe, they introduced their Mediterranean plants to new and fertile territories. These culinary and curative herbs soon found their way into the cultures and cuisines of all the Romans' subjects.

Throughout the Middle Ages, it was the monks and nuns who tended the spiritual and physical well-being of their communities, and herbs found their caretakers in these orders. Not only were cloistered gardens filled with vegetables and indigenous herbs, but new and exotic plants were introduced by traveling monks and pilgrims. Many of these immigrant herbs were described in the ancient herbals that had been secreted away in church libraries, while others were newly discovered plants.

The monks created many of their own herbal beverages and tonics, some to cure the body, many to nurture the spirit. Today, these secret formulas are still enjoyed in sweet liqueurs like Benedictine and Chartreuse.

During the Renaissance, books became accessible to a wider audience because they were no longer written solely in Latin but in vernacular language. With the invention of the printing press, these books found their way into cities and towns, where they were read eagerly. Translations of old herbal texts and a plethora of new titles appeared, and the sixteenth century became known as the age of the herbal. Here was a chance for the people to understand the healing benefits of specific plants and to learn how to minister them. Practical guides illustrated the herbs and often described their other properties, from culinary flavorings to helpful household uses.

One of the most unusual ideas to come out of this era was the doctrine of signatures. It presumed that a plant's usefulness was directly related to its outward appearance. Since an opened walnut resembled a human brain, it was thought to heal a range of brain disorders. Yellow flowers became associated with liver disorders, since jaundice turns the skin a yellowish tint. Ginseng root became a universal cure-all because its shape often resembled the entire human body. It still remains a viable curative.

As North America became colonized by the Europeans, the new immigrants brought along their favorite savory and healing herbs. Kitchen gardens boasted herbs like lavender, rosemary, thyme, sage, basil, and parsley, while many, like chamomile and dandelion, took to the wild.

Herbal teas were abundant, economical, and tasty, but China teas still carried panache—and also a heavy tax from the British government. As patriots began to boycott traditional teas in favor of their own less-expensive herbal blends, the British reacted by flooding Boston harbor with surplus tea. What happened next was the tea party of the century, which helped set the stage for the American Revolution. Over the next decade, "liberty teas" became every patriot's preferred beverage. These brews used herbal combinations to mimic China teas. One favorite was a tea introduced by the native Indians. Called Oswego tea, it was made from the herb bergamot.

Until the eighteenth century, most North American herbs were grown in private gardens, until a religious order known as the Shakers began cultivating herbs on a large commercial scale. Although most were sold as salves and medicines, many were purchased through street vendors and markets as tea and culinary herbs.

With the Industrial Revolution and advances in scientific studies, the use of homegrown herbs and remedies began to wane. Synthetic drugs and flavorings became cultural icons of civilized nations, and the morning call of many families became "Please pass the Tang and the vitamins."

In the last twenty years, there has been renewed interest in herbs. In part, it's a response to the often unpleasant side-effects of artificial ingredients and drugs. And, as the world grows smaller, we're embracing multinational cultures and cuisines and growing increasingly aware of herbs as flavorings and teas.

Beverages are becoming cuisines with a style and reputation all their own. Coffeehouses have menu boards as long as any restaurant's, while British-style tea houses and hotel tea courts list dozens of China and herbal teas. Tea companies and supermarkets are responding to this trend by introducing dozens of specialty herbal blends. In this herbal renaissance, you'll find herbal beverages make a fine complement to a meal, a comforting or stimulating thermos drink to take to work, and the ideal companion for a thoughtful or romantic moment.

TEA AND YOUR WELL-BEING

If you've ever brewed a cup of peppermint tea after an unsettling meal, or sipped some chamomile tea at bedtime just because it tastes good and helps you to sleep, then you've used the natural properties of an herb for their therapeutic value.

Since ancient times, herbs have been used internally and externally in the healing practices of every culture. Today, a majority of the world's population still depends on herbal remedies. Until the mid-1930s, most drugstores in the United States carried mainly herbal preparations and it's still that way in many European countries.

Since the body's healing begins from within, it stands to reason that one of the best ways to use an herb's curative properties is to brew it into a tea and take it internally.

When boiling water is poured over an herb and allowed to steep, the herb's cell walls are broken, releasing its soluble organic compounds and essences into the water and the steam. (That's why your peppermint tea smells so good.) These compounds are what make an herb aromatic as well as therapeutic.

A healthy living plant will release certain of these compounds, known as volatile oils, into the air. This is what we recognize as the scent of a plant, and while we enjoy the aromas, the plants are sending signals. Their oils are either attracting or repelling certain insects, and they also act as antiseptics, to help the plant resist bacteria and viruses.

When you choose to use an herb for its medicinal value, you are using its volatile oils and other organic compounds in much the same way as the plant does, to prevent or counteract an unhealthy situation or, in some cases, to attract an interesting visitor.

Today, many heath practitioners recommend the holistic approach to medicine, using herbs to prevent problems from appearing rather than as a drug to cure them. In either case, when you are using an herb for its medicinal properties, you are using it as a drug and should take proper precautions. Use all herbal teas wisely, and don't try to diagnose yourself without seeing your doctor first.

In the chapter Your Guide to Herbs, you'll learn about the special curative properties of forty well-known herbs and their ability to relieve common ailments. If you are interested in pursuing herbal medicine further, there are many excellent books and practitioners in the field.

How do you say it?

Herb or Erb. Either way is fine.

In the United States it's usually pronounced "erb,"

while in England it's pronounced with the "h,"

as in "Herb, please pass the honey."

Herbal Remedies

While herbal teas can be freely enjoyed without being thought of as medicines, there are various methods used to release an herb's healing properties.

INFUSION is a somewhat formal term for any beverage made by steeping an herb or herbal blend in boiling water. Medicinal teas are steeped longer and are more potent than teas drunk for pleasure.

TISANE is the French word for an herbal infusion. Originally made from pearl barley and barley water, over the years *tisane* has become synonymous with all herbal teas.

DECOCTION is a method used when an infusion will not release the active ingredients because the plant materials are too coarse. Barks, certain seeds, and roots are brought to a boil in water and simmered, and then the liquid is usually reduced by thirty percent.

SYRUPS are made by combining infusions or decoctions with honey or unrefined sugar. They mask unpleasant flavors and are soothing to sore throats.

TINCTURES are made by steeping an herb or blend of herbs in water and alcohol for up to two weeks. Tinctures have a shelf life of up to two years and are taken diluted in warm water or fruit juice.

TONIC WINES are a great way to make the medicine go down. They're created by submerging tonic herbs in good-quality red or white wines and leaving them to steep for a couple of weeks in your refrigerator.

STEAM INHALANTS are created from the steam of boiling water infused with herbs. Breathing the steam is helpful in cases of nasal congestion due to colds and sinusitis.

Gathering Your Own Herbs

YOU HAVE TO BUY most beverages in order to enjoy them. Herbal tea is one drink you can create and make yourself. It's as easy as setting aside a corner of your yard and discovering the world of herbal gardening and the joys of harvesting and drying your own. Today's global markets and cottage industries make your local supermarket, with its aisles of international foods and fresh local produce, a world of herbal pleasures. The herbs you use to make herbal tea come from one of three places: they've been commercially grown, you've grown them in your own garden, or they've been picked in the wild. In this chapter, we'll teach you how to gather the herbs around you. We'll also look at ways to harvest, dry, and store tea herbs.

PURCHASING HERBAL TEAS

Herbal teas are showing up everywhere these days—in espresso bars, local diners, and four-star restaurants. Even fast-food chains are beginning to offer herbal teas and coolers as an alternative to coffee, tea, and soft drinks. Next time you're at the supermarket, look for the tea section. More and more shelf space is devoted to tea companies like Celestial Seasonings, Republic of Tea, Stash, and Tazo, which specialize in quality dried herbal teas. Even Starbucks, the king of caffeinated chic, has herbal blends called Infusia to calm your jitters. It's fun to try these different teas and look over the ingredients listed on the side panel. They're a great source of useful and amusing information. Although it's difficult to duplicate commercial blends, because a dozen or more herbs and essential oils are often used to create a particular flavor and market niche, you'll find many intriguing combinations to try with your own herbs.

When buying dry herbal teas (whether tea bags, loose tea in tins, or bulk teas), buy only enough to drink in three to six months, because once you open the package or tin, the herbs are exposed to air and they'll begin to deteriorate and turn stale. This is especially true if the herbs are dried and minced for uniformity, since more surface area is exposed and they lose their flavor sooner than whole herbs.

In the case of tea bags, where the herbs are finely minced, buy ones that are individually packaged. It's not as good for the environment, but it certainly improves the quality of your cup. (In the chapter Creating Your Own Blends you'll see how easy it is to make your own tea bags so that freshness and environmental concerns are never in question.)

Increasingly, specialty coffee and kitchen stores are offering bulk loose herbal teas. It's an easy way to buy exactly what you want, and to assure quality at the same time. Look for good color and aroma. Loose teas should be stored in air-tight, opaque containers to keep them fresh.

PURCHASING FRESH HERBS

The easiest place to buy commercially grown fresh herbs is in your supermarket. With more emphasis on locally grown produce, many greengrocers have fresh herbs delivered several times a week. If organically grown herbs are available, buy them.

They're usually fresher because they're grown closer to home and they haven't been subject to chemical sprays. Another good herb source is a farmers' market. They're popping up in big cities and suburban towns, with independent farmers bringing in fresh produce to sell. Local neighborhood newspapers often advertise market locations, and most daily regional newspapers feature a weekly food section and hot line. Their staff will know what's happening in their area and they often are aware of additional sources not listed in the paper.

WILDCRAFTING

All herbs grew in the wild until we decided it would be far more convenient to grow them in a garden. Foraging for culinary and medicinal herbs beyond the garden gate is known as wildcrafting.

Before plants were identified and their effects noted, finding out which herbs were tasty, useful, and safe was often a matter of trial and error, too often ending in a deadly mistake. Even when you are armed with the most current scientific information and detailed photographs, mistakes can occur. Wildcrafting is only for the experienced and observant.

If collecting wild herbs is appealing to you, be careful. It's easy to confuse plants. Always use at least two dependable botanical field guides. It's wise to have two opinions, since one description or illustration may not be clear. And, never experiment with an unknown herb. The effects could be harmful or even deadly. It is a commonly told tale in the Pacific Northwest, where foxglove (*Digitalis purpurea*) grows wild, that a woman gathered foxglove leaves, believing they were comfrey. She brewed herself and her husband some tea to soothe their arthritic joints, drank it, and died, since in fact it contained a strong dose of the heart stimulant known as digitalis.

In today's world of pesticides and pollutants, it makes sense to be familiar with the area where you gather herbs. Avoid land that may be contaminated with herbicides, pesticides, or harmful toxins. That covers a lot of territory these days. Raspberry leaves along a country roadside can be covered with exhaust fumes; chamomile used as a lawn or ground covering might be sprayed with chemicals or fertilized.

If in doubt, leave it out. My wildcrafting these days revolves around a large vacant lot that's on my morning walk and excursions with friends who are naturalists. I've seen each season come and go in these places for years. I've watched my favorite "weeds" sprout, grow, and die back and I recognize the flowering chamomile and fragrant lemon balm leaves.

Wildcrafting is still done commercially in many parts of the world, especially for medicinal purposes, and there are herbalists who feel the wild strains are superior in their effects. When you buy wildcrafted herbs and preparations, do so from an established herbalist or health-food store. Many wildcrafted herbs are collected in countries with limited quality control. You want to make sure that the herb you're getting is the one you want.

GROWING YOUR OWN HERBS

Gardening is becoming one of the most popular recreational pastimes in North America, and with it has come a surge in home-grown herbs. Not since World War II with its Victory Gardens has the United States seen more backyard plots and curbside gardens. Other countries and cultures have always used their vacant green spaces for flowers and vegetables, and when space is scarce, have planted creatively. We too can make vertical gardens from hanging containers, trellises, and espaliers, wel-coming potted herbs into any landscape, kitchen windowsill, or balcony corner.

If you have a yard or a vegetable garden, you probably already know how easy it is to grow herbs. In fact, you may have cursed a few as "damn weeds." Most of the herbs we use for tea are pungent herbs native to the dry and rugged Mediterranean coast. Their ancestors were hardy. They had to be in order to survive hot sun, poor soil, and little moisture. Today, their offspring still have the "good bones" of their Mediterranean kin and have been bred successfully to flourish in a wide range of environments and to produce larger plants with a higher percentage of volatile oils.

One of the first things to decide when growing herbs is where you want to grow them. All plants have four basic needs—sunlight, soil, water, and nutrients—but not all plants have equal needs. You'll want to decide which herbs you want to grow and whether you have the right growing conditions for those herbs. The chapter Your Guide to Herbs outlines the optimum growing conditions of the most popular tea herbs. Consider this guide and note the Latin botanical names of the herbs that interest you. That's important, because when you go to buy seeds or plants, the name to count on is the botanical one.

Unless you're planning a naturalized garden where your herbs need to fend for themselves, there's a lot you can do to make your garden a compatible home for your herbal tea plants. Sunlight is basic. Most herbs like full sun, which means at least five hours a day. Set aside the sunniest corner of your garden for your herbs. If a building or tree blocks sunlight to your garden, you'll need to investigate shade-loving herbs.

Herbs grow best in soil where water can pass freely through their root system. You can alter the soil with soil amendments or grow herbs in raised beds and containers with commercial soil. When good soil provides the essential nutrients for healthy plant growth, fertilizers often aren't needed. In fact, fertilizing herbs to produce big bushy plants will give you lots of plant growth, but smaller concentrations of aromatic volatile oils. Use a balanced, organic fertilizer with restraint when you do fertilize.

When it comes to watering, herbs, like any plants, need more when they're growing than when they're dormant. Because their Mediterranean ancestors grew in dry climates, many herbs prefer drier conditions than your flowers and vegetables, so a good rule to follow is to water only when the top few inches of soil are dry.

If you want to learn more about the art of planning and planting a large-scale herb garden, there are many excellent books available. They'll give you step-by-step instructions, from detailed drawings of garden designs to choosing a site and plant propagation. There are also herbal garden specialists who can help with individual needs. The best place to start is your local nursery or parks department. The staff can often put you in touch with garden specialists familiar with your area, its hardiness zone (that's the annual number of frost-free days and minimum winter temperatures), and the herbs that will grow best in your garden.

CONTAINER GARDENING

Whether you have a five-acre spread or a studio apartment, you can grow your own herbs thanks to container gardening. Potted herbs can find their spots anywhere there's light and a few square feet of space. Outside, they will fill a patio, the front door steps, or an empty spot in a garden landscape. If level ground is at a premium, potted herbs can hang from walls and fences, railings, and roof overhangs.

The knack to successful container gardening is to recreate the ideal conditions for herbs growing in the ground. With a little ingenuity, you can create a lush herb garden without worrying about weeds or mowing the lawn. Since most containers are portable, they can move with the sun and the seasons. If your pots are large and heavy, use platforms with wheels to make traveling easier. That way, you can change a balcony landscape, or move fragrant herbs closer to your patio picnic.

One of the charming aspects of container gardening is choosing the container. Because my small garden is located on a balcony, I'm sticking to terra-cotta pots because the herbs overflow with color and texture, and I like the uniformity of brick-colored pots. But container choices are endless: wooden tubs and fiberboard planters; glazed urns and plastic bowls; recycled wine crates; even colorful Italian olive oil tins in the gallon size. Whatever you choose, just make sure it can hold soil and has drainage. One way to vary your containers is to use a terra-cotta or plastic pot as your inside liner. Then, your outside pot can be any charming and artistic covering that you like.

Just as crucial as choosing which container you'll use is deciding which herbs to plant. After noting which plants have similar growing conditions, you can group

herbs however you wish. It might be your favorite herbal tea blends or plants with the same color flowers. An assortment of scented geraniums with variegated leaf shapes makes an eye-catching combination. A large Chinese urn filled with lemon-scented herbs introduces a sweet-smelling focal point. I also like the idea of variations on a theme, so I have a row of eight ten-inch terra-cotta pots, each filled with a single, different type of aromatic mint.

GROWING HERBS INDOORS

If you live in a flat with four walls and some windows, you can grow herbs. In fact, many familiar tea herbs thrive indoors year-round or rotate from patio to garden with the ease of an adaptable guest. And indoor herbal gardening isn't just for city dwellers. For country folk, potting tender herbs like parsley, basil, and tarragon before the first frost and bringing them inside ensures a fresh supply of tea herbs throughout bleak and wintry weather. Some other popular herbs for indoor tea gardens are bay, catnip, chamomile, dandelion, jasmine, lavender, lemon balm, lemon verbena, marjoram, mint, oregano, rosemary, sage, savory, scented geraniums, thyme, wintergreen, and woodruff.

Herbal house plants are attractive accessories to any decorating scheme and freshen the air with their natural perfume. Three thousand years ago, the Egyptian Queen Nefertiti surrounded her chamber with fragrant rosemary- and thyme-filled urns, and the young boy-pharaoh Tutankhamen was very fond of aromatic baths. Modern research shows that indoor plants rid surrounding air of pollutants like benzene and other gases. They do this by absorbing these gases during photosynthesis. These natural air fresheners do away with the need for any sickeningly sweet aerosol sprays.

Indoor plants require the same care as any plants grown in containers, but herbs are particularly well suited to this nomadic and tightly quartered life. In the best of worlds, an indoor gardener is trying to duplicate the outside environment by providing each plant with its optimum light, water, fresh air, and nutrition. In the real world, this isn't always possible, but herbs make the most adaptable house guests. In the chapter Your Guide to Herbs, the growing conditions of the most popular tea herbs are described, so you can decide where best to place your herbs and how to grow them.

Since most herbs are sun-loving Mediterranean natives, a south-facing window that gets light all day is usually the best location, but any compass direction will work as long as the plants you choose grow in that particular light. Just make sure that direct sunlight isn't beating through a windowpane and baking your tender plants.

While the kitchen seems to be a favorite room for potted herbs, look around the rest of your house. A bathroom, a guest room, or the empty floor near the fixed window of a sliding glass door are perfect locations for an indoor garden.

I have a small entry hall with double-hung windows and rows of coat hooks. Every winter it becomes a scented mint and geranium arbor with pots and hanging baskets. The old hall table usually reserved for a pile of keys and afternoon mail doubles as the winter resort for half a dozen potted mints sunning themselves on a tray of river pebbles. In the land of central heating, plants wither from lack of humidity. An easy way to avoid this is to keep the pebbles doused with a little water. Pots will need a non-porous saucer or tray to keep the floor or table from getting damp. I display my herbs on an assorted array of foot stools and children's chairs I've picked up at flea markets. When not in use as herbal pedestals, they're a perfect spot to seat a visiting preschooler or put on a pair of boots.

When you bring an herb indoors, it's best to use a commercial indoor potting soil. It's porous and crumbly, and the water drains easily, preventing root disease or rot. You should water only when the top few inches of soil are dry and use room-temperature tap water to avoid shocking the plant. Right before watering, I give the container a quarter turn so that all of the plant gets equal light and air. Herbs like fresh air like the rest of us, so on temperate days I open the windows and let the breezes flow. Air circulation will keep dust and insects from settling on your plants as well as on your possessions.

When it comes to fertilizing and pest control, I use organic products made for indoor plants. The best place to find these is at a garden center, where you can purchase everything from all-purpose brands to genus-specific items. Some combine both a fertilizer and insecticidal soap. For those who think of their plants as pets, it's a little like picking your favorite pet food: your wallet's the limit.

One problem with growing tea herbs indoors is that you're constrained by the number of plants you can grow and there-fore by the amount you can gather from a single plant and still keep it healthy. A good rule to follow is to pick no more than one fifth of the herb. The way I solve this dilemma is to keep several pots of my favorite tea herbs growing at once. When you want some fresh rose geranium or mint tea—or a combination of both—you take a little from each of several plants and you're ready to enjoy yourself.

HARVESTING HERBS

In the ancient world, herbs were har-vested according to the position of the planets, or in the case of lemon balm, only when music was playing to distract any snakes guarding the precious herb.

Times and traditions have changed, and whether you're snipping herbs from your window box or your neighbor's garden or searching out plants in a vacant lot, any time is the right time to pick an herb if you're in the mood for a fresh cup of tea. But, if you're thinking of harvesting enough to dry for future use or planning ahead for afternoon tea, when and how you gather your herbs makes a difference.

The ideal time for harvesting is on a bright, sunny morning when the dew has dried and the wind is still. That's when the plant's volatile oils are at their peak, before the afternoon sun or wind evaporates them.

The highest level of volatile oils comes after the period of most active growth. For leaves, that peak is just before the plant, or individual stem, flowers. When harvesting leaves, always use clean, sharp scissors or garden clippers instead of pulling them off with your fingers. It causes less injury to the plant. Unless I'm harvesting the whole plant, I take only the newest growth. Think of it as pruning. That way the plant will have a pleasing shape and can regenerate more leaves for future "crops." It's helpful if you have several identical plants growing at the same time. That way you can spread your pickings. A plant will hardly miss a sprig or two.

Flowers are at their peak in the morning when they've just begun to bloom and the heads are fully open. They can be cut with the stem on or off, depending on how you're planning to dry them. Since seeds are the by-products of flowers, you'll need to wait until the flowers fade in mid-summer or early autumn and the seeds are nearly ripe. Herbal roots are gathered when you no longer want the plant, or in the autumn when the aerial parts have died back.

If you've cut back your garden's overgrown mint or bought a bunch of basil when you only needed a small amount, the best way to preserve and savor any leftover fresh herbs is to dry them for future use.

When an herb is dried correctly, its moisture (water) is removed, but its distinctive flavors and aroma (volatile oils) remain. The easiest way to do this is to air-dry the herb in a warm, well-ventilated room that's out of direct sunlight. (The garage is not a good place, because of car exhaust and pollutants.) In the past, I've used an attic, a laundry room, and a child's playhouse. This year, it's the shady corner of my three-sided, high-rise balcony.

The first thing you need to do before drying an herb is to remove any dust, dirt, or insects with a gentle shaking. This is also the time to remove any dead or diseased leaves or stems. If that doesn't do the trick, give your herb a quick wash with cool water. But be sure to pat the water off with a dry cloth or paper towel.

The time-honored way to dry leaves or aerial parts is to cut the stems in small bunches and tie them together with string. (Rubber bands also work.) You'll want the bunches small enough so that the stems

aren't cramped together and so that circulating air can easily reach the drying leaves. Next, suspend the bunches upside down on a nail, peg, or rafter. To save space, try fastening a few bunches from a clothes hanger or from a collapsible drying rack made for clothes. Mint, sage, lemon balm, oregano, and thyme dry easily this way, but watch out for basil. If enough air doesn't circulate around the leaves, they'll turn dark.

If you have time, but not space, pluck the leaves off the stems and dry them in a single layer in a flat basket, on a clean window screen, or on a sweater-drying rack. Once again, make sure that air can circulate around the leaves and that the trays are placed in a warm, dry spot.

This works especially well with larger leaves like mint and sage. For tiny leaves like thyme, dry the entire sprig. Either way, depending on the plant part and moisture content, it will take between twenty-four hours and several days for the herbs to become completely dry so that they crunch when crumpled, but still retain color. If the leaves or flowers have turned brown, they were either dried at too high a temperature or left out too long. Either way, most of the volatile oils have also left, and it's best to start over.

If you're in a hurry, a conventional oven or food dryer will cut down on time. Some people use a microwave, although it only handles small amounts and needs to be watched carefully. To use a microwave, start with the defrost setting (200 watts) for $2\frac{1}{2}$ minutes, and then let the herb "rest" for 10 minutes. If it isn't completely dry, give it another zap.

If you have an electric oven, heat it to a warm temperature (100°F). Check your temperature using a portable oven thermometer, then place your herbs on cookie sheets. Turn the oven off and leave the oven door slightly open. Check periodically until the herbs crumble easily. With a gas oven, the pilot light radiates enough heat to dry most herbs, but drying may take longer than in an electric oven. For food dryers, it's best to follow the manufacturer's directions.

Air or oven drying also works for roots. First wipe the roots clean and trim off any small, woody side roots. (Peeling isn't necessary.) Then spread them out so they don't touch one another and allow them to dry until they shrink and become brittle. You also can tie an individual root on a string and suspend it the same way you dry aerial parts or slice it into manageable pieces and lay the slices to dry in single layers on trays or baskets.

When drying seeds or small flowers like lavender, tie a paper bag over the flowers and hang them upside down. That way, you can catch any seeds and florets as they dry. Give the flowers a mild shaking from time to time to help facilitate the process. It's a good idea to poke ventilation holes along the sides of the bag to keep air circulating. Although flowers can be dried in the same way as leaves, they'll dry more easily if they're cut off the stem and placed in a single layer on a flat, paper-lined surface or tray. When dry, you can remove the petals from the seed head.

STORING HERBS

After you've gone to the trouble of collecting and drying the herbs you'd like to save, here are a few steps to keep in mind when storing them:

❧ Make sure the herbs are absolutely dry.
❧ Store your herbs in clean, clearly-labeled containers away from direct sunlight.
❧ Use leaves and flowers within a year. Seeds and roots will last for several years.

If herbs aren't completely dry, they'll turn musty once they're stored; even one limply dried mint leaf has the power to turn the whole bunch moldy so that your tea tastes like someone's long-forgotten gym socks.

The best storage containers for dried herbs are clean, dark glass jars with screw-top lids or tight-fitting corks. That way, you're able to see what and how much is in the jar, but direct sunlight cannot get through. Ceramic containers are another option, although you can't see what's inside. Clear glass also works, but you'll need to keep your herbs out of the sunlight. In any and all cases, make sure the jars are absolutely dry.

While small jars are relatively easy to find by recycling food jars you've bought at the supermarket, the larger ones are more difficult to locate. Before places like Pottery Barn, Crate & Barrel, and Williams-Sonoma carried large glass jars, I'd buy bulk containers from restaurant or laboratory supply companies found through the Yellow Pages. Another cheap and easy supplier turned out to be a café around the corner from my flat. Their recycled gallon mayonnaise jars made ideal containers for my dried mint leaves and red clover heads. The jars were clear, so I kept them in a closed cupboard.

A word about plastic storage bags: they save space, but over time they'll also impart

What's in a Name?

ALL PLANTS HAVE TWO NAMES. The first is the familiar or common name, which is in English and can change from one area of the country to another. (For example, bergamot is also known as Oswego tea, mountain mint, and bee balm.) The second is the botanical name, which is in Latin and is part of an international system for identifying and naming every plant on earth. The botanical name, which is written in italics, has at least two parts: the genus and the species.

The genus is always capitalized and can include a large number of plants sharing similar characteristics. Different plants within a genus are called species and the species name is

always lower case. The species name often describes the specific plant in some way. (For example, the species name for a scented geranium, or pelargonium, with a lemon fragrance is *Pelargonium limoneum*.)

Sometimes a third name will appear when a species has more than one form but the forms are not distinctive enough to require separate species. The third name is known as a variety and is also in italics. If you find an herb whose third name is not in italics, but has quotation marks around it (such as *Pelargonium odoratissimum* 'Prince of Orange'), it means that particular variety was cultivated by man and not found in the wild.

a dulling flavor or aftertaste. For short-term use, when you're off hiking in the woods or heading down to work, they're a handy way to save space and reduce weight.

To identify each container, you'll find self-sticking labels work best because they don't easily peel off. (This is a virtue that can prove irritating when you want to remove one, but a little vegetable oil or WD40 applied to the unruly label will do the trick.) Write your herb's name and the date it was picked with a permanent pen. Sometimes I'll use two labels, especially if it's a new herb I'm trying or one I don't often use. The front label has the herb's name—that way I can use the same jar for different harvests—and a smaller label on the back has the date it was picked, the amount used for my two-cup pot, and the time I let it brew. One summer, I collected fresh nettle leaves (wearing gloves to avoid the sting) with an herbalist friend. After drying the leaves and brewing a light green tea flavored with honey, I labeled the jar as follows: 8/6/95; 4 tsp; 8 min.

When storing herbs, I find it makes sense to work with only one herb at a time. Although it's easy to tell or smell one herb's leaf from the next when it's fresh, herbs become much more mysterious when dried and often reveal their true identity only in boiling water. In the dried state, all thyme is created equal.

The less you tamper with your dried herbs, the better the flavor will be. So, if space permits, try to preserve whole leaves, seeds, and roots. If it's necessary to store in pieces, keep them as large as possible. Remember, the more surface area exposed to the air, the greater the chance aromatic oils will evaporate. Grinding or pulverizing a herb may save space, but you'll end up with a less satisfying brew. This applies not only to herbal teas, but to culinary herbs as well. Don't you think it's time to throw out all those little jars and tins of herbal confetti that have been hiding in your cupboard for months?

If you like the idea of having fresh herbs year-round, there are many herbs that freeze well and bring you the taste of summer. Mint, basil, and lemon balm leaves freeze best if taken off the stem, while rosemary and thyme work best if left on. As with any preserving, make sure the leaves are clean and dry before placing them in labeled freezer bags. When it's time to brew, just take out the amount you need, reseal the bag, and immediately put it back in the freezer. It's surprising how fast leaves will thaw when left out on the counter.

Small freezer bags are ideal for single-pot, two-cup servings. If you have a favorite fresh herb blend, place all the ingredients in a labeled bag so you're ready at a moment's notice to make your favorite infusion. (For a brilliantly refreshing tea, try 1 cup spearmint and ½ cup lemon balm mixed with ¼ cup sage.) Small freezer bags also come in handy for iced summer drinks. By freezing herbal tea in ice cube trays and then storing the cubes in labeled bags, you'll have these frozen gems ready for double duty, either as tasty ice cubes to cool a summer tea or combined in a blender with frozen fruit to make a delicious slush.

Preparing Your Own Cup

THERE ARE MANY WAYS to prepare a delicious cup of herbal tea. You can gather wild herbs and steep them over an open campfire, brew a pot of afternoon tea with a ready-made tea bag, or make an evening nightcap using your own homemade blend. ❧ Whatever way you choose, brewing a delicious cup of herbal tea is easy. All it takes is a container, some boiling water, and your herb of choice. But if you're regularly brewing tea, you'll find there are some basic utensils that are quite helpful: a kettle for boiling water, a teapot for brewing and serving, an infuser or strainer for removing the herbs, and a cup to savor your creation. ❧ While herbal tea is simple to make, the following steps will assure you success with every cup. This chapter presents each of those steps with other useful information that will help you make a delightful brew every time.

USE CLEAN UTENSILS

To get the best, most tantalizing cup of herbal tea, your utensils need to be clean. If they aren't, the chance you'll end up with a satisfying brew are slim.

Even if your kettle is used only for boiling clean water, it still can become dirty and take on an unpleasant aftertaste. This is usually the result of mineral deposits and other debris that collect after constant use, so it's important to periodically clean your kettle.

Frequently, a light scrubbing with a non-abrasive sponge or soft brush and a good rinsing will do the trick. If not, simply apply a small amount of baking soda or a mild, unscented detergent to a sponge or brush, wipe the inside surfaces, then thoroughly rinse with clean water.

When you're buying a kettle, make sure the lid is removable for easy cleaning. You could be surprised by some electric models and "looks-are-everything-designs" that don't have lids and are filled through the spout. This is courting disaster. After a few months of constant use, who knows what lurks down that dark abyss.

Teapots come in all shapes and sizes and are made of china, earthenware, glass, or metal. Some have built-in strainers to hold the tea ingredients; others need a ball-shaped infuser or a hand-held strainer to remove the herbs from the brewed tea. It's best to use a china, earthenware, or glass teapot because they're easy to clean, retain heat, and won't impart a metallic taste.

Some tea lovers have a teapot for every occasion. Others keep one for China tea and one for herbals. I have an old English brownstone I use every day for every kind of tea. If you like all types of tea as I do, remember, teas made from *Thea sinensis* (China tea) and certain herbs will build up a tannin residue on the inside of your teapot if it's not clean. (That's the brown stain you might have noticed clinging to the sides and imparting to any tea you brew a bitter undertone.)

Check to make sure your teapot lid fits well. If you see steam seeping around the lid or if you're enjoying the aroma of your tea while it's brewing, you're losing some of the volatile oils to the air when they could be savored in your cup. (Remember, it's the volatile oils that give your herbal tea an appealing taste and many of its healing properties.)

A tea infuser, also known as a "tea egg" or "tea ball," is a perforated metal container that holds the herbs you've measured in your teapot or cup. There are also ceramic infusion baskets. Bamboo or metal strainers are another way to keep the herbs out of your cup of tea. These implements clean easily with water and only occasionally need a dunking in soapy water. Bamboo may need to be replaced more often as it stains with use and absorbs flavors if it's used to strain strongly flavored teas.

A word about your teacup. If it feels good in your hand, comfortable to your lips, and pleasing to your eye, return the favor by keeping your cup clean. After all, it promises a world of future pleasures.

USE COLD, GOOD-TASTING WATER

Most people use tap water to brew their tea. It's fast, convenient, and easy to reach. But if it's been chemically treated, has an odor or an aftertaste, the delicate taste of your herbal tea will suffer.

Remember, if the water doesn't taste good, neither will your tea. If you have any doubts, here's an easy way to check: turn on the tap water and let it run briefly. Fill a glass halfway with room-temperature water and place a small saucer over the lid. With the lid in place, swirl your glass (imagine you're at a restaurant about to taste a fine glass of wine) and remove the lid. Immediately place your nose as close to the water as possible and take a good sniff. Does it smell like your neighbor's swimming pool or a favorite fishing creek? Now, take a sip and let it roll around on your tongue. Is it bitter or medicinal? When you make ice cubes from your tap water, do they have an unpleasant taste or smell?

If any of the answers is "yes," try using bottled or filtered water. There are several self-filtering pitchers on the market that are inexpensive and simple to use. Brita is one manufacturer. Distilled water is another option, although it has a flat taste that many people dislike.

If you're using cold tap water, be sure and let it run a short time before filling the kettle. The first water out of your tap has been sitting in the water pipes for several hours or overnight and will taste flat because it's lost some of its oxygen. And don't be tempted by the hot water tap. You won't save any appreciable time in heating the kettle water and the water may have been stored in the hot-water heater for hours.

After your kettle of water is on the stove, preheat your teapot with warm water. When it's time to brew, simply pour the water out of the teapot and add your herbs. I also like to warm my cup by swirling a little hot water inside it.

USE THE CORRECT
BREWING METHOD

After deciding what kind of herbal tea you're going to brew, you'll be choosing one of two brewing methods, either infusion or decoction.

If you're using leaves, flowers, or certain seeds, you'll make an infusion. It's the most common way to make tea and usually involves brewing in a teapot. When making an infusion, bring fresh water *just* to the boil in your kettle. Place the herbs either directly in the warmed teapot or in a tea ball or infuser and add the hot water. Then allow the mixture to steep, so the herbs are thoroughly saturated for a certain period of time. This gentle steeping allows the volatile oils to be released into the water without evaporating. After the herbs steep, remove them, and sit down to enjoy what you've just created.

When bark, roots, or certain seeds and berries are used, you'll brew by making a decoction. It's the method most often used for medicinal teas. Because these plant materials are tougher and it's more difficult to release their volatile oils, you place them in a saucepan with cold water and bring them to a boil. Allow the mixture to simmer until the liquid is reduced by one-third. Then remove the herb and serve the tea. In the case of medicinal teas, where doses are taken throughout the day, the tea can be kept in a covered jug or pitcher and sipped hot or cold.

With either infusion or decoction, one specific herb or several herbs can be brewed at a time, as long as the method corresponds to the specific plant part you are using. You can also make a potent combination by straining a hot decoction into a teapot holding herbs ready for infusion. This way you can easily make a tea from roots and leaves. Tea made by either or both methods can be enjoyed hot or iced.

In the chapter Creating Your Own Blends you'll have a chance to try some delicious herbal tea recipes that use the methods just described. In the chapter Your Guide to Herbs you'll learn which method is best for forty of the most popular herbs used in making tea.

When making conventional China teas (*Thea sinensis*), it's easy to get a consistently good cup using exact measurements, because only the leaves are used. Brewing an herbal tea requires a little more ingenuity since you're using different plant parts. (Good-quality packaged herbal teas and tea bags have reliable directions.)

If you're using fresh herbs, remove any imperfect or damaged leaves or flowers. It's not necessary to cut or mince the herbs, unless you're using a measuring spoon or trying to fit them into an infuser, but always bruise the leaves with your fingertips to break down their cell walls and help release the volatile oils. Dried herbs also release their oils more easily if pinched or crushed between your fingers before you place them in your teapot or infuser.

When using seeds or roots, crush them slightly to release their oils. A mortar and pestle or an electric coffee grinder works nicely, and a rolling pin will crush seeds or roots wrapped in a muslin towel or cloth. I use a smooth, pear-shaped stone I found on a hike in Bellagio, Italy, years ago. Besides being a great tool in the kitchen, it brings back lovely memories.

As a general rule, when you are making an herbal infusion or tisane, use 1 rounded teaspoon of dried herb, or 3 rounded teaspoons fresh, for every cup (8 ounces) of freshly boiling water. In the case of seeds, use $1\frac{1}{2}$ teaspoons for 1 cup or 1 tablespoon for every pint (2 cups). If you're using a tea ball or infuser, make sure not to fill it too full because the herbs need room to expand as they absorb water. When making tea for a crowd or an extra-strong brew for iced tea, I use 2 balls to give the herbs lots of soaking room.

A decoction is mainly used for bringing out the healing properties of coarse plant materials like roots, stems, and bark, and the amounts are frequently measured in ounces. Usually a decoction calls for $\frac{1}{2}$ ounce of the dried root or bark, or 2 tablespoons of seeds, for every pint of water. (To weigh herbs, small digital kitchen scales can be purchased for under thirty dollars through catalogs and kitchen and department stores. They're also great for weighing pasta and postage.)

Generally, the highest-quality herbs with the best flavor come from freshly dried or homegrown herbs. Herbs that you've properly grown and nurtured or collected yourself will always have a fresher edge and superior volatile oils. The chapter

Gathering Your Own Herbs describes the steps you can take to assure that the herbs you grow are the best they can be.

When purchasing dried or fresh herbs, rely on reputable retailers and judge the quality of their herbs the same way you would judge your own, by checking the color and seeing how the herbs are stored. (See Mail Order Sources, page 104, for stores that sell dry herbs.) Fresh herbs often can be found in your grocery store's produce section. Get to know your green-grocer for the inside scoop on when the fresh herbs arrive.

BREW TEA AT THE CORRECT
WATER TEMPERATURE

Because of the subtle and delicate flavor of most herbal infusions, it's best to use water that has *just* come to the boil. Water that's at a rolling boil will evaporate the herb's volatile oils with its steam. And, because there's less oxygen in the water, your tea will taste flat.

In decoctions, it's also essential to bring the water *just* to the boil and then to turn down the heat and let it simmer so that the herb's soluble contents have time to steep. Again, you don't want to create a lot of steam and lose the oils.

MAKE SURE THE BREWING
TIME IS CORRECT

Unlike most China teas, herbal teas don't always become darker the longer they steep. So you'll need to rely on your sense of taste and past experiences instead of using your eyes to tell when your beverage is ready.

The general rule for an herbal infusion is to start by steeping for 5 minutes. However, you'll find that some herbs, like lavender, may give you the flavor you like after infusing for only 2 to 3 minutes. Others, like chamomile, may require up to 10 or 15 minutes.

When making a decoction, the tougher plant parts will need to slowly simmer for 10 to 15 minutes, or until the liquid is reduced by one-third.

The first time you brew a particular herb, you're really experimenting to see what strength brew you like best. It may take a couple of teapot trials to decide. Don't forget to write down the amounts and brewing time, so you can repeat your successes and not your mistakes.

Once your tea is brewed and ready to serve, remove the herbs by lifting out the tea ball or tea bag or by straining the contents directly into a cup. In the case of a decoction, you may wish to strain the tea into a warmed teapot before serving.

An item you may find useful is a padded tea cozy. It insulates your teapot and keeps the contents hot for up to thirty minutes. I also have a two-cup thermos I keep just for my herbal teas. That way, if I'm taking a drive or just don't want to get up from my desk, there's hot tea close at hand.

But the last step is the most important one of all: give yourself time to enjoy the tea you've created. Stretch out in the sun; lie back and listen to the rain; or, better yet, share your tea with a friend.

IN THE LAND OF MILK AND HONEY

The delicate and varied flavors in most herbal teas often eliminate the need for any additional sweeteners. But sometimes a drizzle of honey or molasses just feels right and brightens your cup. That's one of the nice things about an herbal tea. It can be enjoyed by itself, and it also loves the company of other flavors. (Recipes for some unusual herbal sweeteners are included at the end of the chapter Creating Your Own Blends.)

For a change, try adding some orange zest or a sliver of ripe plum. Try other fruits. Fresh juices can be added the same way milk is added to coffee.

Speaking of milk, it has been a popular additive to coffee and China tea since the seventeenth century. It was believed that adding a small amount to the cup before the hot tea was poured would prevent fragile china cups from cracking. You may find a teaspoon or two of milk will smooth a pungent herbal taste and make it less astringent. This is especially true in teas made from berry leaves which have tannins. (Tannins are chemical compounds present in many plants and give traditional tea its body.) There's a reason milk, not cream, reacts this way. It contains a protein called casein that binds with the astringent tannins to give your tea a mellower taste.

Iced Pleasures

TRY MAKING HERBAL ICE CUBES with your leftover tea. Mint and

lemon balm tea ice cubes make a delightful addition to traditional iced teas. For a

festive touch, try freezing a fresh leaf or petal garnish in each ice cube.

Creating Your Own Blends

FOR THOUSANDS OF YEARS, herbal teas have been appreciated for their healing powers as well as their pleasing tastes. The first herbal teas were probably simple combinations of an aromatic herb and water or of a less-savory herb with curative features. It didn't take us long to figure out that "if one is good, two must be better," and we began mixing herbs to combine their tastes and talents. ❧ When any herb is brewed and sipped by itself, it's known as a simple or self-drinker. A refreshing cup of peppermint tea is a widely enjoyed self-drinker. ❧ When two or more herbs are combined, it's known as a blend. Over the last five years, the world of herbal teas has expanded, with new combinations showing up on market shelves and restaurant menus. Tea companies are constantly experimenting and blending dozens of herbs, spices, and natural flavorings to create flavors and special home remedy blends that appeal to the consumer.

If you grow or collect your own herbs, you already realize that creating your own blend is one of life's intriguing pleasures. While I often stick to familiar, homemade or ready-made blends in the winter, I look forward to the summer when I experiment with my herbal garden at its peak. First thing Saturday morning, I go out with my teapot and loosely fill it with what I see or smell. One day it might be sprigs of lemon verbena and lemon balm with a few peppermint leaves tossed in; other mornings, several sprigs of thyme might be joined with a single sprig of rosemary and spearmint. I improvise, but over the years I've come to know which individual flavors I like and what goes well together.

Once you become familiar with the individual flavors and tastes you like, you can begin sampling two-herb and multi-herb infusions, herbs with fruits and juices, and herbs with traditional China teas. When you discover a blend you like, be sure to write down the recipe or formula.

Instead of listing ingredients in teaspoons, tablespoons, or cups, we often use the term, "parts." Parts refer to *equal* amounts; that way you can brew by the tablespoon, the cup, or the pound. For example, if an herbal recipe calls for 1 part peppermint leaves, 1 part sage leaves, and 2 parts lemon balm leaves, it can mean: 1 tablespoon peppermint leaves, 1 tablespoon sage leaves, and 2 tablespoons lemon balm leaves; or, 2 cups peppermint leaves, 2 cups sage leaves, and 4 cups lemon balm leaves. These proportions will work in as small or as large a quantity as you like.

When using a blend of fresh herbs to brew tea, place them directly in your teapot or infuser or dry them. Dried blends can be placed directly in the pot or infuser, or you can put them in tea bags you make yourself. Most herbal tea suppliers carry strips of ready-to-seal tea bags. All you do is drop a teaspoon of your herb or herbal blend into each bag, hold the strip shut with a ruler, and iron the open edge to seal. (The typical cost is $3 for 50 bags.) Another alternative is to use *bouquet garni* bags, especially when you're serving a crowd or making an herbal bath blend. They're small, reusable muslin bags, approximately 2 by 4 inches, and typically have an orange drawstring. (The average cost is $1.80 for 8 bags.) Homemade herbal tea bags can be made by cutting 2-inch muslin squares, placing 1 to 2 teaspoons of herbs in the center of each square, and tying it with string into a small bundle.

The following pages will give you ideas and recipes to try on your own. You may want to begin by sampling some of the two-herb and multi-herb blends I've listed and recommend after half a lifetime of experimenting. Or, you may want to try herbalist Patti Chambers's favorite morning brew. There's even a recipe for *chai,* the ancient Indian beverage that is currently captivating the coffee and cappuccino crowd. And, if you feel like adding a little extra sweetness to your tea, I've included several recipes for herbal syrups and honeys.

Most of the suggestions and recipes are made with ingredients you can easily find in your garden, herb shop, or the market. Any ingredients that are difficult to find can be ordered through the sources listed in the last chapter.

TWO-HERB BLENDS

Here is an introductory list of herbs that go well together. Begin by making a cup or a pot using equal parts of each herb. Right away you'll discover what you like and don't like, and if you want more of one herb than another. Two-herb blends are an easy and inexpensive way to gain confidence in your own creative abilities, and most of the time you'll be rewarded with a tasty beverage. Once you've found a two-herb blend you like, try adding a third, perhaps a spice. If the blend is good but too strong for your liking, think of diluting it with fresh juice or seltzer water. Below are a number of two-herb blends that are the favorites of herbal tea enthusiasts.

Bergamot and sweet cicely
Chamomile and apple mint
Chamomile and hibiscus
Chamomile and lemon balm
Lemon verbena and mint
Marjoram and mint
Mint and ginger
Pineapple sage and lemon verbena
Rose geranium and mint
Rosemary and ginger
Rosemary and hibiscus
Rosemary and lavender

When you use more than two herbs, you begin to recognize the special nuances each herb has to offer and how it interacts with other herbs to create a unique taste. It's a little like perfume. Every fragrance has its own signature and aroma. Sometimes one particular "note" stands alone; at other times, it's a harmonious blend. What you like is a matter of personal preference. The following list will help you create your own tempting melody.

Applemint, spearmint, and orange mint
Basil, lemon balm, and cloves
Basil, lemon thyme, and lemon verbena
Bergamot, fennel seeds, and ginger
Catnip, chamomile, marjoram, and spearmint
Chamomile, lemon verbena, spearmint,
and rose petals
Hibiscus, lemon verbena, and rose hips
Lemon grass, rosemary, and thyme
Peppermint, lemon grass, and rose hips
Spearmint, sage, and lemon balm

Herbal Tea Recipes

Here are several special recipes created by people who know and love herbal teas: Patti Chambers, Claire Archibald, Juanita Crampton, and Steven Smith.

PEPPERMINT AND CHAI SPICE TEA

In India, *chai* is a traditional tea that blends exotic spices and black tea with boiled milk and water to create an invigorating beverage refreshing to body, mind, and spirit.

Juanita Crampton, one of the creators of Sattwa Teas, a line of exotic commercial *chai* teas in the Northwest, created this special herbal mix and tea for your enjoyment.

1 cup milk
2 teaspoons Peppermint and Chai Spice Tea Mix (recipe follows)
1 tablespoon granulated sugar
1 cup water

In a small saucepan, combine the milk and water and bring to a boil. Reduce the heat to low and stir in the tea mix. Remove from heat and steep for 5 minutes. Strain into a pitcher and stir in the sugar.

Makes 2 servings.

Peppermint and Chai Spice Tea Mix
4 tablespoons dried peppermint leaves
4 tablespoons ground cinnamon
3 tablespoons ground cardamom
3 tablespoons ground ginger
1 tablespoon ground cloves
1 tablespoon ground black pepper

In a mixing bowl, blend together all of the ingredients. Store in covered container with a tight-fitting lid until ready to brew.

Makes 1 cup dried tea or 48 servings.

This aromatic tea is the creation of Patti Chambers, one of the Northwest's most engaging and enthusiastic herbalists and teachers. She lives on a quiet acre called Herb House, located on the Pine Lake Plateau in Washington. In the spring, when her garden comes alive with fresh young leaves and flowers, she brews this flavorful tea each morning for herself and her husband Paul.

10 fresh purple sage leaves
16 fresh lemon balm leaves
12 small mint leaves
Petals of 1 red rose
2 rose-scented geranium leaves (optional)
6 cups freshly boiling water

In a pre-warmed, 6-cup teapot, place the sage leaves, lemon balm leaves, mint leaves, rose petals, and geranium leaves (if using). Pour in the freshly boiling water, and let the tea steep for 10 to 20 minutes.

Makes 6 servings.

In Mexico, Agua de Jamaica (pronounced "hah-my-ca") is served to celebrate any happy occasion. It's also become a favorite street vendors' beverage, served alongside colas and orangeades. While there are many powdered "instants," there's nothing like the real thing.

In McMinnville, Oregon, Claire and Shawna Archibald own a destination spot called Cafe Azul, and Claire is their innovative chef. On opening day, Agua de Jamaica was presented to all the guests and still appears as a welcoming drink.

2 packed cups dried hibiscus flowers
8 cups water
1 cup granulated sugar
Additional water, if necessary

In a saucepan, combine the hibiscus flowers with 6 cups of water. Bring to a boil and simmer gently for 5 minutes. Remove from the stove and mix in the sugar. Cool and strain the liquid into a large pitcher. Add the remaining 2 cups water to make 2 quarts. Adjust sugar to taste. To serve, pour over ice.

Makes 2 quarts.

During a recent visit to the Herbfarm's nursery and four-star restaurant in Issaquah, Washington, I had the pleasure of taking an herbal tea class from Patti Chambers. She welcomed each of us with a freshly brewed cup of rosy tea that had a fragrant lemon-spice aroma. No wonder her students keep signing up for classes.

½ cup dried hibiscus flowers
½ cup dried rose hips
½ cup dried lemon verbena leaves
½ cup dried peppermint leaves
½ cup dried orange peel

Place the ingredients in a large mixing bowl and stir until well blended. Store in a dry, air-tight container in a cool, dry place. To use, measure 1 tablespoon for each 8-ounce cup of freshly boiling water. Steep for 10 minutes.

Makes 2½ cups dried tea or 24 servings.

This tea is a delicious way to bring your day to a close, but keep in mind tea master Steven Smith's advice: "Put on your jammies before taking your first sip."

2 teaspoons cut, dried mint leaves
1 teaspoon dried chamomile flowers
1 heaping teaspoon cut, dried catnip leaves
½ teaspoon cut, dried valerian root
1 teaspoon dried, crushed hops
3 cups (24 ounces) freshly boiling water
Honey, to taste (optional)

Take a small plastic bag and place inside it mint leaves, chamomile flowers, catnip leaves, valerian root, and hops. Blow into the bag as if blowing up a balloon. Once it's inflated, hold the bag shut and shake until herbs are well combined.

Place mixture in a pre-warmed teapot and pour in boiling water. Let the tea steep for 10 minutes. Strain. Pour into cups and add honey, if desired.

Makes 3 cups.

Steven Smith is the founder, tea master, resident shaman, and storyteller at Tazo, a Northwest tea company with a complete line of dry and microbrewed bottled teas, all of them refreshingly different. His golden brew Seer combines the delicate, unfermented taste of a China green tea known as Young Hyson with three fragrant and stimulating herbs. Smith not only knows it tastes great, but tells me that after I savor a cup, my mind will be sharper and my thoughts more insightful.

> 3 teaspoons cut, dried Young Hyson or
>   Gunpowder leaves
> 1 teaspoon cut, dried lemon verbena leaves
> ½ teaspoon cut, dried lemon grass
> 1½ teaspoons cut, dried spearmint leaves

Take a small plastic bag, and place inside it Young Hyson leaves, lemon verbena leaves, lemon grass, and spearmint leaves. Blow into the bag as if blowing up a balloon. Once the bag is inflated, hold it shut and shake until the herbs are well combined. (When mixing herbs for his own use, Steve finds this unorthodox method is quick and easy.) For each serving, steep 1 teaspoon of the dry ingredients in 8 ounces of just-boiling water for 5 minutes.

Makes 6 servings.

Sweet Herbal Syrups and Honeys

HERBAL SYRUPS

Whether your beverage is hot or cold, a simple sugar syrup will give it a uniform sweetness. By infusing the syrup with aromatic herbs, you can add interest and further embellish your drink. Here are two easy recipes with suggestions for many other combinations. When frozen, many flavored syrups make delicious herbal sorbets.

ZEFIRO'S GINGER SYRUP

Zefiro, a highly celebrated and intriguing restaurant in Portland, Oregon, is known for its innovative menus. Simple, elegant, fresh flavor and taste are the keys. The owner and chef, Chris Israel, uses this easy ginger syrup to make ginger-based drinks.

A dash adds a spicy zest to herbal teas. It also makes the base for a delicious home-made ginger ale when seltzer or carbonated water is added.

> 2 cups water
> 2 cups thinly sliced, fresh unpeeled ginger root
> 2 cups granulated sugar

Place the water and ginger in a small saucepan. Bring the mixture to a boil and remove from heat. Let the mixture steep for 1 hour. Strain the ginger slices, reserving the water, and pour the water back into the saucepan. Add the sugar and bring the mixture to a boil, stirring until the sugar dissolves. Remove from heat and cool. Keep any unused syrup refrigerated in a covered container and it will last several weeks.

Makes 3 cups.

Variation:
To make a natural ginger ale, add 1 ounce of the ginger syrup to a tall glass. Add 12 ounces of seltzer or carbonated water. Serve with ice.

MINT SYRUP
WITH ORANGE ESSENCE

In the summer, I like to make a fresh mint syrup to sweeten herbals teas and other warm-weather beverages. When I want a sweet, fruity taste, this combination hits the spot.

2 cups water
1 cup granulated sugar
6 sprigs fresh peppermint leaves
Zest from 1 small orange

In a small saucepan, combine the water and granulated sugar. Heat the mixture over medium heat and simmer, stirring occasionally, until the sugar dissolves. Add the peppermint sprigs and orange zest. Bring the mixture just to a boil, remove from heat, and let the mixture steep for 20 minutes. Strain and chill overnight.

Makes 2½ cups.

Note:
To flavor a simple sugar syrup (1 part sugar, 2 parts water) with any fresh herb or spice, add the herb or spice to the hot sugar syrup and infuse for at least 10 minutes or up to 12 hours, depending on how easily the herb gives up its flavor. Fresh mint, ginger, rose-scented geraniums, and lavender will take 15 to 20 minutes. Sweet cicely and lemon balm may need an overnight soaking.

HERBAL HONEYS

It's simple to create herbal honeys out of your favorite aromatic herbs. One way to discover your favorite single or blended herbal honey combinations is to start small. Here's a basic recipe for two 8-ounce jars. If you like what you make, you can always think big and multiply the amounts.

2 eight-ounce jars honey
1 tablespoon dried lavender flowers
7 fresh rose-scented geranium leaves
5 fresh orange mint leaves, optional

Empty the two jars of honey into a small saucepan and heat over medium heat until hot but not boiling.

Meanwhile, place the lavender flowers in 1 jar. In the other jar, place the rose-scented geranium leaves and the mint leaves. Pour the hot honey back into each jar and seal. Be careful. If the honey is too hot, it may bubble over. Label the exact ingredients on the lids with a permanent pen and keep the jars sealed for 1 to 3 weeks. Taste for flavor.

When ready, strain the herbs by heating the opened jars slightly in your microwave (or setting the jars in a bowl of very hot water for several minutes) and pouring the honey through a sieve and into 2 clean jars.

Makes 2 jars.

Variations:
The following herbs and spices make delicious flavored honeys: cardamom, lavender, orange mint, peppermint, pineapple mint, rosemary, sage, scented geranium, spearmint, and thyme. A teaspoon or two of dried hibiscus or rose hips will add a reddish hue to the honey.

It's not What You Say,
   It's How You Serve It.

EVERY HERB AND FLOWER has a symbolic meaning and you can brew your own herbal blend to make your own eloquent statement with herbs. For dear friends and lovers, the combinations are deliciously evocative, witty, and very personal. Traditionally, the following herbs are identified with these qualities:

Angelica *inspiration*	Lavender *devotion*
Anise *change*	Lemon balm *sympathy, regeneration*
Basil *hatred*	Marjoram *joy*
Bergamot *virtue*	Mint *warm feelings*
Borage *bluntness*	Parsley *merriment, festivity*
Calendula *hopelessness, grief*	Raspberry *remorse*
Chamomile *wisdom, patience*	Rose *love, passion, purity*
Clover *think of me*	Rosemary *remembrance*
Cloves *dignity*	Sage *esteem, wisdom, goodness*
Dandelion *prophecy, foretelling*	Scented geranium *happiness*
Fennel *grief, endurance, power*	Sweet woodruff *humble spirit*
Hibiscus *grace, beauty*	Thyme *daring, courage*
Hops *injustice*	

Your Guide to Herbs

WHETHER YOU GROW YOUR OWN PLANTS
or use ready-made tea bags, this.chapter is intended to give you a closer look
at the plants we often choose when brewing an herbal tea. The first section
details a number of the most popular tea herbs, explores their lore and history, and tells how best to grow and harvest them. You learn what part and
how much of each herb to use in your tea and what its special medicinal properties are. The precise brewing method is described, along with other interesting facts. The chapter's second section gives you a thumbnail sketch of
other plants that can be used for tea, and the last section describes spices that

can be used to make or flavor tea.

Some of these herbs may surprise you. Take basil, for example: it seems more at home in pestos and pastas than in your favorite demitasse. But after a heavy meal, basil's minty, clovelike flavor quickly settles a queasy stomach. And what about your roses, sweet geraniums, and ubiquitous dandelions? Next time you're pruning your garden or digging for weeds, think about turning your cuttings into a pleasing afternoon tea.

Although certain flavors have been universally described, the way a tea tastes is really a matter of opinion. Because herbal teas have a delicate flavor, their subtleties may be difficult to identify. In the end, what is important is how it tastes to you. The chapter Creating Your Own Blends gave you ideas on which herbs taste good by themselves and helped you create your own herbal blends. This chapter helps you identify herbs that heal, soothe, and invigorate.

For over five thousand years, herbal teas have been brewed for their medicinal qualities. Some cures are based on legends, but many have a basis in scientific research. You'll read about each herb's ability to cure common ailments and discover that a remedy for a disagreeable dinner or stuffy nose may be as close as your spice cabinet or balcony garden.

Popular Plants for Herbal Tea

Angelica	Marjoram
Anise	Mint
Basil	Oregano
Bergamot	Parsley
Borage	Raspberry leaf
Calendula	Rose
Catnip	Rosemary
Chamomile	Sage
Dandelion	Scented geranium
Fennel	Sweet cicely
Lavender	Thyme
Lemon balm	Wintergreen

Other Plants for Herbal Tea

Anise hyssop	Lemon verbena
Ginseng	Lime (Linden)
Hibiscus	flowers
Hops	Red clover
Horehound	Sweet woodruff
Lemon grass	Valerian

Spices for Tea

Cardamom	Ginger
Cinnamon	Nutmeg
Cloves	

Popular Plants for Herbal Tea

ANGELICA

Angelica archangelica

In the seventeenth century, angelica appeared in a dream to a ministering monk as the cure for plague. Children around Europe wore the aromatic herb woven in necklaces to ward off the disease, while the juice from its root was believed to cure many infirmities, including old age. According to Christian legend, angelica's flowers bloom every May 8 to celebrate the feast day of the Archangel Michael, and the herb's Latin botanical name commemorates that event.

TASTE: A sweet licorice flavor with celery undertones.

SPECIAL PROPERTIES: The leaf tea can stimulate a sluggish appetite and help digestion, and is also sometimes used as a urinary antiseptic to treat cystitis. The root tea is prescribed for coughs due to colds or the flu. Note: Angelica is considered safe to drink in small doses, but there have been studies that suggest it is inadvisable to drink it in large quantities.

PARTS USED FOR TEA: The leaves. The root and seeds are also used for medicinal tea.

BREWING METHODS: Infusion for leaves. Decoction for root or seeds. For an infusion, use 3 teaspoons of the fresh leaves, or 1 teaspoon dried, in 1 cup (8 ounces) of freshly boiling water. Steep for 5 to 10 minutes, or to taste. Sweeten with honey or sugar. For a decoction, use 1 teaspoon crushed root or seeds to each cup of boiling water and simmer for 20 minutes.

HOW TO GROW AND HARVEST: This tall biennial rivals Jack's giant bean stalk. The hollow stems grow easily five to eight feet in height and are round with grooves like celery. The apple-green leaves appear on long stalks that grow from a sheathed base, and each leaf is divided into three-part, serrated leaflets. Honeybees love the fragrant white flowers that bloom in umbrella-like clusters.

Angelica grows best in moist, rich soil

Bergamot

Angelica

Calendula

Borage

and partial shade. Because of its height, the herb is popular as a background plant in shaded gardens. It grows best from new seeds that are planted in the fall after they've first matured. Self-sowing plants are one of the best ways to increase your supply, and although it's not a commonly-stocked nursery plant, I've always been able to locate a few plants by asking my local nursery. Angelica is classified as a biennial, but if the flower stalk is cut before flowering, it will survive several years. The only problem is you won't have any new seedlings the following spring.

Gather the leaves in the early summer before the plant begins to flower. Between July and September is the best time to harvest the seeds. In autumn, dig up the root when the plant has died back. (To speed up drying, the root should be sliced.) This is one plant that's best not harvested in the wild because it resembles water hemlock which is very poisonous.

OTHER USES: From the root to the seeds, every part of this herb has a delicious use. The stems are often candied and enjoyed as a sweet or as a garnish on pastries and cakes. Ground fine, the seeds or root add an interesting note to muffins and baked goods.

Fresh leaves make a fragrant, edible garnish and an unusual addition to salads. You can also use the dried leaves in potpourris, herbal pillows, and sachets.

ANISE

Pimpinella anisum

Ancient Romans knew the value of anise and chewed on the seeds to keep their breath clean. In the seventh century B.C., Hippocrates recommended anise to cure a cough. A century earlier, the great mathematician Pythagoras thought that by holding an anise sprig one could prevent epilepsy attacks. This herb was so valued in biblical times, it could be used to pay taxes.

Aniseed oil is used as a flavoring in foods, medicines, and cosmetics. It's also quite attractive to dogs. In fact, in greyhound racing, the fake hare the dogs chase around the track is often rubbed with aniseed oil.

TASTE: A sweet licorice flavor. Especially good with honey and milk.

SPECIAL PROPERTIES: Anise tea aids in digestion and makes a soothing bedtime drink to encourage sweet dreams. Aniseed tea helps calm a cough or an irritated throat.

PARTS USED FOR TEA: The leaves and seeds (aniseed).

BREWING METHODS: Infusion for leaves. Decoction for root or seeds. For an infusion, use 3 teaspoons of the fresh leaves, or 1 teaspoon dried, in 1 cup (8 ounces) of freshly boiling water. Steep for 5 to 10 minutes, or to taste. For a decoction, crush or grind 1 heaping teaspoon of aniseeds for each cup of boiling water. Simmer for 5 to 10 minutes.

HOW TO GROW AND HARVEST: This one- to two-foot annual resembles Queen Anne's lace and prefers sunlight and well-drained soil. It grows well from seed or from a cutting, but the young plant doesn't like to be transplanted once it begins to grow.

The leaves are best gathered before the plant flowers. Its seeds are harvested between July and September, after the flowers have bloomed.

OTHER USES: The fresh, tender leaves make a tasty addition to salads and a garnish to shellfish. The gray-brown seeds are delectable in cakes, cookies, and breads. If freckles are a nuisance, try a masque of ground aniseed and watch them fade away. Chewing aniseed is a home remedy for curing the hiccups.

BASIL

Ocimum basilicum varieties

Even though the ancient Greeks used basil as a culinary herb, they thought it was an evil plant with the power to bring misfortune wherever it grew. In order to germinate the seeds, they stamped and cursed the ground they planted.

In other cultures, basil has been well received: the Hindus considered it holy; in Tudor England, pots of basil were a welcome gift to any household; and in French cafés and on pioneer porches, pots of basil added a dash of color and discouraged flies. Today, it's revered—just ask any restaurant reviewer. Chefs from New York City to Catalina Island are crushing those aromatic leaves into pestos, pastas, pies, and punches.

TASTE: Clovelike flavor with a peppery, mint-like undertone.

SPECIAL PROPERTIES: Basil is part of the mint family and, like any of its cousins, makes a soothing tea for nausea. Tea made with the fresh leaves also helps fight depression, especially when combined with lemon balm and rose petals.

PARTS USED FOR TEA: The leaves.

BREWING METHOD: Infusion. Use

In medieval England

ladies embroidered sprigs of thyme,

a symbol of courage, on scarves for their

knights to wear during a joust.

3 teaspoons of the fresh leaves, or 1 teaspoon dried, in 1 cup (8 ounces) of freshly boiling water. Steep for 10 minutes, or to taste. Sweeten with honey.

HOW TO GROW AND HARVEST: This aromatic annual loves hot weather and grows readily from seed. It likes a rich, well-drained soil and a sunny, sheltered location, but will also grow in partial shade. In many gardens, the herb is planted next to tomatoes to discourage fruit flies. To encourage leaf growth, pinch back the young shoots or small white flowers that appear in spikes at the end of each stem.

There are ornamental as well as fragrant basil varieties, with leaves ranging from soft lime green to dark maroon and deep purple. Their different fragrances remind you of a well-stocked spice cabinet with aromas ranging from anise to cinnamon and lemon.

The best time to gather the tender, shiny leaves is before the plant begins to flower. I often cut long sprigs and place them in a blue glass vase beside the kitchen sink. Not only does the fragrance keep me washing dishes more contentedly, but the leaves stay fresh and often begin to root. Basil leaves are easy to dry, but can turn dark if improperly dried or frozen.

OTHER USES: A classic in many cuisines, especially Italian, Mediterranean, and Thai, basil is also used commercially in flavoring mouthwashes, toothpastes, and perfumes.

BERGAMOT

Monarda didyma

A North American native, bergamot is also known as bee balm or Oswego tea. It was a favorite beverage of the Otsego (also called Oswego) Indians in what is now known as New York state. During the American Revolution, patriots drank Oswego tea instead of the heavily taxed British tea as an enjoyable form of protest. It was also during this time that a British general by the name of Earl Grey mixed some of his black China tea with bergamot and came up with the blend that now bears his name. Today, Earl Grey tea gets its flavoring from the bergamot orange, but you can make your own by using your favorite black tea and adding fresh or dried bergamot leaves.

TASTE: A fragrant, sweet citrus flavor.

SPECIAL PROPERTIES: This pleasing tea helps soothe a cough or sore throat, reduces nausea, and eases menstrual cramps. The volatile oils contain an ingredient called thymol, which acts as an antiseptic.

PARTS USED FOR TEA: The leaves and the flowers.

BREWING METHOD: Infusion. Use 3 teaspoons of the fresh leaves or flowers, or 1 teaspoon dried, in 1 cup (8 ounces) of freshly boiling water. Steep for 10 minutes, or to taste.

HOW TO GROW AND HARVEST: A perennial, bergamot is a showy garden plant with brilliant flower clusters ranging from pink and lavender to a deep red. A member of the mint family, the plant has square and erect stems and reaches a height of one to three feet. The dark-green, ovate leaves are three to six inches long and grow opposite each other on the stem. This hardy herb likes moist soil and both full sun or partial shade.

Harvest the leaves before the plant flowers. You can gather short sprigs or cut the entire stem to within 1 inch of the ground, then strip the leaves and lay them on screens or baskets to dry. If this is done before the first flowering, you can usually get a second growth before fall.

OTHER USES: As a culinary herb, the young leaves and bright flowers are a citrusy accent to fresh salads and cold soups. The leaves and flowers dry easily, and since the flowers retain their color, they make a bright addition to wreaths and potpourris. Their fragrance blends well with other herbs in sachets and herbal pillows.

BORAGE

Borago officinalis

From hollowed horn to crystal chalice, many drinking vessels through the ages have been graced by borage's fresh cucumber taste. Ancient Greeks, Celtic warriors, even the Crusaders drank wine laced with borage because they believed it brought courage in battle, plus a sense of well-being. Perhaps that's the reason the British still garnish their vodka-laced Pimm's Cup with the star-shaped blossoms.

TASTE: A cooling, cucumber-like taste.

SPECIAL PROPERTIES: Since a borage leaf infusion helps reduce fever and acts as a mild expectorant, it's often sipped when a flu or cough is coming on. Traditionally, it's combined with fennel to stimulate milk production in nursing mothers.

PARTS USED FOR TEA: The tender leaves, but you can also use the flowers.

BREWING METHOD: Infusion. Use 3 teaspoons of the fresh herb, or 1 teaspoon dried, in 1 cup (8 ounces) of freshly boiling water. Steep for 5 to 10 minutes, or to taste.

HOW TO GROW: This two- to three-foot annual self-sows readily and can often be spotted in empty lots and along sunny roadsides. Tiny white hairs or bristles cover its hollow stems and large leaves. Delightful to honey bees, the sprawling plant makes a lovely addition to any garden, with its blue, star-shaped flowers tipping downward at the end of each stem.

The young leaves can be harvested throughout the growing season, and the flowers are picked when in bloom.

OTHER USES: With its cucumber-like taste, borage is a popular culinary herb. The leaves and stems are added to soups and stews for flavoring, and, like a bay leaf, removed before eating. Fresh flowers can be added to salads for flavor and color; crystalized borage blossoms, made by "painting" fresh flowers with an egg white and dipping into superfine sugar, are an elegant garnish to cakes and petits fours.

CALENDULA

Calendula officinalis

Also known as pot marigold, this flowering herb has always been a garden favorite. Its genus name, *Calendula,* came from the Romans, who observed that in their warm Mediterranean climate the colorful blooms were present every month of the year.

TASTE: Slightly pungent.

SPECIAL PROPERTIES: As a home remedy, calendula tea is suggested for gastritis, and a warm gargle can be used to soothe canker sores. The tea is also recommended for women with painful menstruation or menopausal problems. The petals are useful in coloring a tea blend that may otherwise be clear or uninteresting.

PARTS USED FOR TEA: The petals.

BREWING METHOD: Infusion. Use 3 teaspoons of the fresh petals, or 1 to 2 teaspoons dried, in 1 cup (8 ounces) of freshly boiling water. Steep for 5 to 10 minutes, or to taste.

HOW TO GROW AND HARVEST: This leafy annual likes full sun and well-drained soil and is easily grown from seed. Its ray-shaped flowers, pale yellow to bright orange, bloom from early spring through autumn frosts. If winters are mild, it may continue to flower. Fine hairs cover the stems and leaves, and the entire plant reaches about eighteen inches in height.

When you harvest the flowers, pinch them off the stem and separate the petals. Whole flowers with stems can be dried by hanging them upside down in small bunches, but the petals tend to curl and won't be as visually pleasing.

OTHER USES: Nothing brightens a landscape like a constellation of calendulas in full bloom. They add color to any arrangement and, since they dry easily, can be used in potpourris, wreaths, and dried arrangements. In chic restaurants, the separated petals are scattered in salads, soft cheeses, and sweet breads as a garnish that adds tang. Ground calendula blossoms can be used as a substitute for saffron when you want saffron's color but not its flavor.

For a stimulating bath, try adding calendula blossoms. Or, you can cool an infusion and use it as a hair rinse to bring out highlights in brunette or blond hair. Herbalists use the blossoms in creams and compresses designed to treat localized skin problems due to infection or physical trauma.

CATNIP

Nepeta cataria

Jungle cats and suburban mousers all agree on one thing: a few sprigs of catnip are better than a roll in the hay any day. We too enjoy catnip's subtle, lemony, mint-like flavor. This is the tea the British drank before China tea came to their isles.

TASTE: Minty.

SPECIAL PROPERTIES: Catnip tea is a traditional cold and flu remedy. Because it's a member of the mint family, it soothes an upset stomach. It also has a calming and quieting effect that's especially nice before bedtime, either in a cup of tea or as a soothing addition to your bath. (See Herbal Teas for Healing and Pleasure, page 100.) Catnip closely parallels the effects of valerian, right down to its feline appeal.

PARTS USED FOR TEA: The leaves.

BREWING METHOD: Infusion. Use 3 teaspoons of the fresh herb, or 1 teaspoon dried, in 1 cup (8 ounces) of freshly boiling water. Steep 5 to 10 minutes, or to taste.

HOW TO GROW AND HARVEST: If you have cats, plant this perennial herb out of their reach. Hardy, except for when it comes to feline assaults, catnip resembles mint with its branching stems and scalloped leaves. It will grow two to three feet tall in good, all-purpose soil.

OTHER USES: Ask any cat. Catnip's volatile oils are feline ambrosia, so the dried leaves make an irresistible stuffing for cat toys of all shapes and sizes. As a culinary herb, catnip imparts a pleasant, minty flavor.

CHAMOMILE

Chamaemelom nobile, Roman or English chamomile; *Matricaria recutita,* German chamomile

To the ancient Egyptians, chamomile was a universal remedy, curing chills and fits and assuring everlasting life. The Greeks called it "ground apple," and it's easy to understand why once you've trampled across this low-growing herb in a meadow or a cracked sidewalk—or strolled across the famous chamomile lawn at Buckingham Palace.

TASTE: A light, sweet, applelike taste and aroma.

SPECIAL PROPERTIES: An infusion of the daisylike flowers relieves nausea and, when taken before bedtime, promotes sleep and relieves anxiety. Chamomile tea is also comforting if you're in the throes of a cold. Inhaling the steam made from a double-strength infusion helps relieve nasal stuffiness. (Note: Because the tea is made from flower heads that contain pollen, some people may have an allergic reaction.)

PARTS USED FOR TEA: The flowers.

BREWING METHOD: Infusion. Use 3 teaspoons of the fresh flowers, or 1 teaspoon dried, in 1 cup (8 ounces) of freshly boiling water. Chamomile is one herb that can be enjoyed after steeping for either a short time (3 to 4 minutes) or as long as 30 minutes. For medicinal effects, steeping for at least 25 minutes is recommended.

HOW TO GROW AND HARVEST: This small perennial grows just about anywhere. It likes full sun and will tolerate most soils. Because it spreads readily—the stems can root themselves—chamomile makes a fragrant ground cover or lawn-like surface that makes mowing a pleasure.

The solitary, daisylike flowers should be harvested when the silver-white petals begin to turn back toward the stem.

OTHER USES: Chamomile's applelike scent is popular in potpourris as well as in perfumes. An infusion cooled to room temperature brings out blond highlights when it's used as a hair rinse.

DANDELION

Taraxacum officinale

For many of us, it was the first plant we learned to identify. What child hasn't made a wish by blowing on the dandelion's fluffy seed head? As adults, many people consider it a pesky weed, but connoisseurs value the lowly dandelion for both its medicinal and culinary uses.

Its common name comes from the French *dent de lion,* or "lion's tooth," which aptly describes the deeply notched shape of the leaves.

TASTE: Bland to grassy with bitter undertones. Combines well with peppermint.

SPECIAL PROPERTIES: Dandelion tea is brewed mainly for its therapeutic use as a mild laxative and diuretic.

PARTS USED FOR TEA: The tender, young leaves and the root, mainly used for medicinal purposes.

BREWING METHODS: Infusion for the leaves. Decoction for the root. For an infusion, use 3 teaspoons of fresh leaves, or 1 teaspoon dried, in 1 cup (8 ounces) of freshly boiling water. Steep for 10 minutes, or to taste. For a decoction, use 4 ounces of fresh root or 1 ounce ground dried root in 2 cups (16 ounces) boiling water. Simmer, reducing to 1 cup, then strain.

HOW TO GROW AND HARVEST: This hardy perennial herb with its yellow flowers thrives even in poor soil and is found just about anywhere in the earth's temperate regions. While it's often destroyed as a weed, dandelions can be grown from seeds or wildcrafted.

OTHER USES: In today's chic restaurants, tender dandelion leaves are showing up with other "wild greens" on the salad menu. In many parts of North and South America, the root is harvested, roasted, and ground to be brewed as a coffee substitute, with a taste much like chicory's.

The milky sap from fresh plants helps to eliminate warts, while the flowers are used by weavers to dye their wool yellow.

FENNEL

Foeniculum vulgare; F. vulgare dulce

As long as people enjoy overeating, they'll look for a way to lose weight. The Greeks thought they'd found their elixir in fennel and called it *marathron,* or "to grow thin." During the Middle Ages, the seeds were taken to church services and chewed as a way to keep stomachs from rumbling. (It also makes the breath quite pleasant.) Now that we have diet clubs and lite cuisines, fennel continues to be appreciated as a digestive herb with a sweet licorice flavor.

TASTE: Anise with peppermint undertones.

SPECIAL PROPERTIES: A cup of fennel tea after a meal aids digestion and decreases intestinal gas. It relieves baby's colic and helps nursing mothers increase their milk flow.

HOW TO BREW: Infusion for seeds and leaves. For seeds, slightly crush 1 heaping teaspoon of the seeds for every cup of freshly boiling water. Steep for 10 minutes. For leaves, use 3 teaspoons of fresh leaves, or 1 teaspoon dried, in 1 cup (8 ounces) of freshly boiling water. Steep 5 to 10 minutes, or to taste.

HOW TO GROW AND HARVEST: A close relative of dill, this semi-hardy perennial grows four to six feet in height, flourishing in rich, composted soil and in a warm, sunny location. Fennel sends up its erect, hollow stems from a thick, bulbous base. Its feathery leaves are dark green, and its small, yellow flowers are perched at the tips of an umbrella-like flower head.

Fennel dislikes being transplanted, so it's best to plant the seeds or young plants exactly where you want them to grow. But be advised: if you are planting fennel in a vegetable garden, don't put it near your tomatoes or bush beans because it has an adverse effect on their growth.

You can harvest fennel leaves at any time. They shrink and become quite delicate when dried, but freeze nicely. When the flowers begin to change from golden green to brown, cut off the entire seed head and place it in a paper bag to dry so that you can collect the seeds.

OTHER USES: Fennel finds most of its uses in the kitchen. Every part is edible, from the root to the seeds, and each imparts a delicate anise flavor. Fennel seeds are popular in all kinds of baked goods and savories. (Try to imagine the rich and deliciously spicy taste of Italian sausage without the fennel.) *F. vulgare dulce,* also known as Florence fennel, is the variety whose bulbous base is most often found in supermarkets and in culinary dishes. Instead of jicama or radish in a salad, try slicing a Florence fennel bulb with fresh avocado and sliced oranges.

LAVENDER

Lavandula spica, L. vera, L. angustifolia, L. officinalis

From nursery rhymes to lovers' knots, lavender has long been one of the world's favorite herbs. Since ancient Roman times, the aromatic flowers have scented baths and given fragrance to perfumes and potions.

The word lavender may be derived from the Latin *lavare,* "to wash." In the Middle Ages, women tucked sprigs of lavender between their freshly laundered sheets.

Happily, that's a habit still practiced among devoted lavender lovers.

TASTE: Slightly sweet, highly aromatic flavor. Used as an accent in herbal blends.

SPECIAL PROPERTIES: Long considered a medicinal plant, lavender relieves fatigue and depression and tension headaches. Lavender blends well with rosemary as a treatment for depression, and with valerian as a treatment for headaches.

PARTS USED FOR TEA: The flowers.

HOW TO BREW: Infusion. Use 2 teaspoons of fresh flowers, or 1 teaspoon dried, in 1 cup (8 ounces) of freshly boiling water. Steep for 5 minutes. (If you prefer a weaker brew, experiment with using less lavender.)

HOW TO GROW AND HARVEST: Easy to cultivate in a pot or a plot, this perennial shrub has narrow silvery or gray-green leaves and spikes of tiny fragrant flowers. The plant will grow from seeds or cuttings, although seeds are difficult to germinate. Young cuttings and mature bushes are easy to find in most garden centers, and there are many varieties from which to choose. Lavender likes to grow in well-drained soil in a warm, dry, sunny spot. We're not the only ones to find this plant alluring; it's a favorite among butterflies and honey bees.

The flowers are harvested at the peak of their bloom. An easy way to gather the drying petals is to cut and tie a bunch of stems together and place them inside a paper bag with a few holes poked in the sides for air circulation. Hang upside down to dry.

OTHER USES: Popular in blended potpourris and sachets, dried lavender gives towels and bed linens a fresh, clean scent when placed between stacked sheets. To give your bath a refreshing and fragrant aroma, use large, *bouquet garni*–sized tea bags filled with lavender. It's the perfect way to forget that the weekend's almost over. (See Creating Your Own Blends, page 43.)

Lavender's smooth, pungent leaves are used as a culinary seasoning in some *herbes de Provence*, Southern France's equivalent of a *bouquet garni* for soups and stews. Lavender flowers and their infusions are used with delicious results in condiments and desserts.

LEMON BALM

Melissa officinalis varieties

Also known as balm or sweet balm, this lemon-scented herb has provided comfort and pleasure for hundreds of years. The ancient Greeks believed it cured dog and

scorpion bites and used it to flavor wine; colonial Americans found it made delightful tea; and Thomas Jefferson made sure he included it in his garden at Monticello. *Melissa* is the Greek word for "bee," and lemon balm is a favorite of honeybees.

TASTE: Lemony and invigorating.

SPECIAL PROPERTIES: When you're suffering from a cold or the flu, sip a soothing mug of lemon balm tea to ease stuffiness. A warm brew also soothes nerves and aids digestion. Because it acts as a mild vasodilator, lemon balm tea is believed to help lower blood pressure. Breathing a steamy infusion is good not only for a stuffy cold, but may help acne.

PARTS USED FOR TEA: The leaves. Fresh leaves give the best flavor.

BREWING METHOD: Infusion. Use ¼ cup of fresh leaves, or 1 teaspoon dried, in 1 cup (8 ounces) of freshly boiling water. Steep for 5 to 10 minutes, or to taste.

HOW TO GROW AND HARVEST: Best grown from cuttings, this hardy, one- to three-foot-tall perennial likes sun to partial shade and will do well in most soils. The light-green, heart-shaped leaves grow abundantly along the stems, and the tiny, white flowers appear where the leaf meets the stem.

Gather the leaves before the flowers bloom. If you decide to dry the leaves, it's best to lay them flat on trays or screens.

OTHER USES: Shakespeare suggests in *The Merry Wives of Windsor* that lemon balm leaves make a great furniture polish. He's right; the volatile oils in the leaves will polish wood and leave a lemon scent.

In the kitchen, fresh leaves make a nice addition to fruit, chicken, green salads, chilled soups, and marinades when a slightly lemony flavor is wanted. (Don't mince too far in advance because the cut leaves tend to discolor.) Lemon balm is also an ingredient in at least two liqueurs: Chartreuse and Benedictine.

Fresh sprigs of lemon balm add greenery and scent to any bouquet, and the dried leaves are also used in potpourris, sachets, and herb pillows. Fresh or dried leaves will make your bath a fragrant, sweet-scented time-out.

MARJORAM

Origanum marjorana

According to Greek myth, marjoram was used by Aphrodite to heal a wound from Eros's arrow, but instead of curing her pangs of love, the sweet herb only increased her passion. That's one reason the ancient

BETTER THAN A CAT

Mice and other rodents don't like

the smell of mint. One way to keep them away from your pantry

is to scatter dried or fresh sprigs in the cupboard.

If fleas are a problem, scatter a few sprigs of pennyroyal.

In your garden, mint will repel aphids and flies.

Greeks and Romans would weave the wiry marjoram stems into bridal crowns.

In medieval times, marjoram leaves were rubbed on furniture because the volatile oils left not only a sheen but a lovely fragrance. And, before hops were used in brewing beer and ales, marjoram was the flavoring of choice.

Also known as sweet or knotted marjoram, this herb is closely related to wild marjoram or oregano (*Origanum vulgare*). Their history and uses are often intertwined.

TASTE: A sweet flavor resembling a blend of thyme and sage. The longer it steeps, the more pungent it becomes.

SPECIAL PROPERTIES: New England settlers drank a warming cup of sweet marjoram tea to help relieve tension headaches and mild coughs. It's still used that way today.

PARTS USED FOR TEA: The leaves.

BREWING METHOD: Infusion. Use 2 teaspoons of fresh leaves, or 1 teaspoon dried, in 1 cup (8 ounces) of freshly boiling water. Steep for 5 to 10 minutes.

HOW TO GROW AND HARVEST: A Portuguese native, this tender perennial with its small, velvety, gray-green leaves is often treated as an annual since it survives only the mildest winters. The small, foot-high bush has stems covered with small hairs. Slow to germinate from seeds, marjoram grows most easily from purchased seedlings or cuttings. This herb loves full sun and a light or medium-rich, well-drained soil.

Fresh leaves can be harvested at any time, but it's best to pick them just before the flowers appear.

OTHER USES: A familiar kitchen herb in Portuguese, Italian, and French kitchens, marjoram's flavor goes well with many cuisines. It makes up part of the classic *bouquet garni* used to flavor soups, stews, and broths and is an essential flavoring in certain German sausages.

Sweet marjoram is a popular choice for herbal bath mixtures because it scents the air and helps relax sore and tired muscles. The French use it in sachets, like lavender, to scent their linen.

MINT

Mentha species

In an early Greek myth, Persephone, the queen of the underworld, became impatient with her husband's wandering eye, especially when Hades noticed a young nymph named Minthe. One day, in a fit of jealousy, she turned the lovely woman into mint. Armed with this story, Hippocrates warned men to use mint cautiously because too much caused impotence.

Today we think it's somewhat chic to find a mint sprig spiking our dinner water, but the Greeks and Romans made it a daily habit, not only in their drinking water but in their bath water as well. Slaves drank mint-flavored barley water as a thirst-quenching tonic.

In medieval times, the fresh-smelling herb was tossed on floors and trampled to sweeten stale rooms, and tables were rubbed with the leaves to make dining more pleasant.

TASTE: Cool, refreshing and, depending on the variety, a highly characteristic undertone. The accent flavors range from peppermint and spearmint to apple, pineapple, and orange.

SPECIAL PROPERTIES: A popular home remedy, peppermint tea helps lift the spirit as well as calm an upset stomach. All mints aid in digestion and relieve nausea, especially due to motion sickness. They're also useful for headaches and tension. Women who suffer painful menstrual cramps find mint tea helpful as a relaxant. An infusion of milk and mint leaves is a tasty variation.

Because peppermint (*M. piperita*) is more potent medicinally than other mints, spearmint (*M. spicata*) is used more often in children's tea. Research also suggests that pennyroyal (*M. pulegium*) should not be regularly used as an herbal tea. The oil contains a chemical that's been shown to induce menstruation. If you're a woman, stick to peppermint and spearmint as your herbal tonics.

Inhaling the steam of a double-strength herbal infusion will help relieve nasal congestion. Mint tea can also be used in compresses to soothe itching and inflammation.

PARTS USED FOR TEA: The leaves, often a whole sprig.

BREWING METHOD: Infusion. Use 3 teaspoons of fresh leaves, or 1 heaping teaspoon dried, in 1 cup (8 ounces) of freshly boiling water. Steep for 5 to 10 minutes, or to taste.

HOW TO GROW AND HARVEST: This Mediterranean native has been a garden herb since the pharaohs' time and will grow almost everywhere, although it prefers moist, partially shaded areas.

There are over a hundred varieties, but the most common garden mint is spearmint. An invasive perennial, mint spreads by creeping underground stems that send up erect branches. Its identifying feature is its square stem, which can reach two feet in height. Run your finger along the branching stem and you'll never fail to recognize mint again. The fragrant, green leaves grow opposite each other on the stem with serrated edges.

The best way to get new plants for your garden is by cutting lengths of the underground stem and replanting it, or by buying a cutting from a nursery. (Although peppermint is sterile, some mints will grow from seed.) Because mint spreads so rapidly, many herbal fanciers suggest sinking the mint in its container in the ground to keep the roots from spreading. This works for two or three years, but then you'll need to dig it up and cut back the plant.

It's best to harvest the leaves just before the flowers open.

OTHER USES: As a flavoring for mouthwash, toothpaste, chewing gum, candy, and medicine, it's number one. But there are as many uses for mint as there are varieties. Peppermint, the main flavor ingredient in crème de menthe, is used by engineers to test pipe joints because its volatile oils will betray any leaks.

From flavoring sauces to perking up a fruit salad, fresh potatoes, or peas, mint is a handy herb to have in the kitchen. It adds flavor to an extraordinary number of recipes.

Stems of flowering mint add color and life to floral bouquets and their dried leaves make a fresh accent to potpourris, sachets, and herb pillows.

In your garden and your teapot, these sweet-scented mints will bring you pleasure: peppermint (*M. piperita*); spearmint (*M. spicata*); apple mint (*M. suaveolens*); pineapple mint (*M. suaveolens 'Variegata'*); Corsican mint (*M. requienii*).

OREGANO

Origanum vulgare

This adaptable plant is a Mediterranean native. A close cousin to marjoram, oregano (or wild marjoram) was highly prized as a medicinal herb for centuries, but it didn't find its way into the kitchen cupboard until the eighteenth century.

TASTE: Fragrant, somewhat bitter taste, stronger than sweet marjoram and with a balsamic undertone.

SPECIAL PROPERTIES: A mild tonic, oregano tea also aids in digestion and reduces colic and gastric discomfort. Certain herbalists recommend oregano tea in the early stages of measles, believing it causes the patient to perspire and the eruptions to appear.

"I Like My Parsley Crisp."

Well, if that's the case, take the advice of a sixteenth-century

English herbalist and stuff a

tennis ball with parsley seeds.

After a few good bounces—

or a mediocre game—

the seeds will be well bruised and ready to germinate.

When the first leaves appear, press them down to the ground

and the next to arise will be as crisp as you please.

As a gargle or mouthwash, an infusion of 3 teaspoons dried herb steeped in 1 cup freshly boiling water will help to relieve a sore throat. Let the tea cool until it is warm to the touch before using.

PARTS USED FOR TEA: The leaves.
BREWING METHOD: Infusion. Use 2 teaspoons of fresh leaves, or 1 teaspoon dried, in 1 cup (8 ounces) of freshly boiling water. Steep 5 to 10 minutes, or to taste.
HOW TO GROW AND HARVEST: A native of Greece, this perennial is hardier than marjoram and can withstand harsher conditions. The small, one- to two-foot-high plant sprawls as it grows. Like marjoram, its stems are covered with small hairs, but oregano's small gray-green leaves are larger and coarser.

Before purchasing a young plant, taste one of the leaves. The flavor will differ depending on variety and sub-species. Note the Latin name on the plant you prefer so that if you decide to grow it from seed, you'll know what to buy. This herb does well in full sun with well-drained soil.

To harvest, cut sprigs before they begin to flower. Oregano may be cut back drastically without injuring the plant.
OTHER USES: What's spaghetti sauce without oregano? This versatile culinary herb is now a part of many cuisines, from Italy and Greece to Cuba and Mexico. It enhances egg dishes, marinated vegetables, stews, and vegetables. If you run out, you can always substitute marjoram, although you'll need to use more since it has a milder flavor.

PARSLEY

Petroselinum crispum

Today's favorite dinner plate garnish has a sinister history. The ancient Greeks dedicated this aromatic herb to the queen of Hades, Persephone. The annual emergence of the goddess from the underworld signaled the arrival of spring, and so her plant, parsley, was also the Greeks' symbol of spring. They believed that the seeds visited the nether world nine times before sprouting—maybe that's why it takes so long to germinate—and they placed parsley wreaths on tombs to honor the dead. Because of this association, the early Greeks didn't use it as a culinary herb, although the poet Homer describes Greek warriors feeding their chariot horses fresh parsley to give them courage and strength in battle.

First-century Romans knew a breath-sweetener when they tasted it. After a meal heavy with garlic and onion, they chewed parsley as we would suck a breath mint. On festive evenings, parsley garlands were worn as crowns or necklaces in the belief that the herb would absorb any wine fumes and keep the party-goer from becoming drunk.

TASTE: It tastes the way it smells, with a fresh and cooling undertone.

SPECIAL PROPERTIES: One of the best sources for vitamin C, parsley tea is used as a mild diuretic. It is also prescribed as an infusion to relieve indigestion and to induce or hasten menstrual flow.

As a caution, it's best to avoid drinking this tea during pregnancy because strong, medicinal infusions can stimulate contractions.

PARTS USED FOR TEA: The leaves. The roots and seeds are also used in making medicinal infusions.

BREWING METHOD: Infusion. Use 2 teaspoons of fresh leaves, or 1 teaspoon dried, in 1 cup (8 ounces) of freshly boiling water. Steep 5 to 10 minutes, or to taste. Fresh or frozen leaves make a better-tasting tea than dried leaves.

HOW TO GROW AND HARVEST: A biennial, parsley grows well from seeds in rich, moist soil and in a partially shaded spot. The feathery leaves are bright green with serrated edges that lie flat or curl depending on the variety.

Gardeners often use parsley as a border plant and will sow it three times a year to get a continuing supply: once in early February, if ground and weather permit; again in early May; and for the third time in late July.

The leaves can be harvested any time, but the tender, young leaves make the best tea. Some prefer only the leaves from the first year's growth; the second year's leaves may have a bitter aftertaste.

OTHER USES: Fresh parsley makes a striking arrangement when partnered with bright roses or other garden flowers.

Parsley is believed to be poisonous to birds and parrots, but sheep and rabbits thrive on its leaves. In nineteenth-century England, it was thrown into ponds to keep the fish healthy.

RASPBERRY LEAF

Rubus idaeus

The raspberry plant's luscious berries tend to attract our attention, but the leaves have played an important medicinal role for centuries. Raspberry leaf tea has been a mainstay in the herbal medicine cabinet, helping to ease morning sickness and childbirth.

TASTE: Astringent and dry, raspberry

leaves are often used in conjunction with other herbs to make blended teas.

SPECIAL PROPERTIES: The tannin in the leaves relieves diarrhea and is also used as a diuretic. Because of its reputation as an ease to childbirth, herbal teas blended with raspberry leaves are often prescribed for pregnant women. Raspberry leaf tea also makes a soothing gargle for sore throats and canker sores.

PARTS USED: The leaves. The berries make a delicious juice or wine. Dried leaves can be purchased easily through herbal stores and suppliers. (See Mail Order Sources, page 104.)

BREWING METHOD: Infusion. Use 2 teaspoons of fresh leaves, or 1 teaspoon dried, in 1 cup (8 ounces) of freshly boiling water. Steep 5 to 10 minutes, or to taste.

HOW TO GROW AND HARVEST: This perennial herb is generally grown by taking suckers from the plant, although it grows well from seeds. The prickly canes can reach seven feet in height and like full sun and deep, well-drained, loamy soil. The green leaflets grow in clusters. The small white flowers, followed by the tasty, crimson fruit, appear during the second year's growth.

Raising berry canes is more complicated than growing tender herbs. Consult your nursery for the best varieties in your region and take its advice on growing and care.

To harvest, clip the young tender leaves that grow in the spring and summer before the fruit ripens.

ROSE

Rosa species

From a dozen long-stemmed red roses to a single, perfect bud, the rose has always been a symbol of love—for those wise enough to know that love combines great beauty with sharp thorns.

Have you ever noticed the plaster ornament that often decorates the center of a Victorian ceiling? It's known as a "rose" and recalls an earlier custom: fastening a rose over the dining room table as a sign that all conversation would be held in confidence.

For aroma and tonic qualities, any scented, deep red rose is well suited for teas. The best rose hips come from a wild rose known as the dog rose (*Rosa canina*).

TASTE: The petals make an exotic brew that, depending on the rose variety, can be highly aromatic. The hips have a pleasant, fruity taste that's mildly tart and astringent.

SPECIAL PROPERTIES: Ounce for ounce, rose hips are higher in vitamin C

To prevent nightmares in ancient

Rome, a fresh sprig of rosemary was placed

under a fretful sleepyhead's pillow.

than an orange. It's the tea to take when you're fighting a cold or whenever you need more vitamin C. The petals of *R. gallica* make a tea that is soothing to a sore throat, especially when combined with sage leaves. The Chinese make a decoction with the flower buds of *R. rugosa* to help with digestion and as a tonic for the blood.

PARTS USED FOR TEA: The petals and the "false" fruit or hips.

BREWING METHOD: Infusion. Use 2 teaspoons of fresh petals, or 1 teaspoon dried, in 1 cup (8 ounces) of freshly boiling water. Steep 5 to 10 minutes, or to taste. The rose hips can be ground in a coffee grinder and infused, using 1 teaspoon to each cup of freshly boiling water. (If you want to preserve the vitamin C, use hot but not boiling water.) Steep for 5 to 10 minutes.

HOW TO GROW AND HARVEST: Whole encyclopedias have been written about the care and cultivation of roses. For the beginning or amateur gardener, it's a good idea to invest in some general and specific garden books. Armed with that knowledge and a good nursery, you'll be able to find and grow just the right roses. You can grow roses from seeds or cuttings, but I've always used nursery-grown stock (or transplanted a few from my mother's garden).

Depending on the variety, roses grow from several inches to many feet. While most are shrubs, there are also creeping and climbing varieties. Flowers, which come in almost every color but blue, may appear as solitary blooms or in clusters, with as few as five petals or up to several hundred.

Before harvesting the petals or the rose hips, make sure the plant is free of pesticides. Petals are best when gathered before the flower is completely open, then carefully separated from the stem. The rose hips are collected in the early autumn. (The real fruit is inside the fleshly red receptacle called the hip.)

OTHER USES: Most people associate roses with bouquets and perfume. Attar, the essential oil of the rose, is found in over 96 percent of all women's perfumes. (In the world of perfume, rose attar holds a "base note," which means it is still detectable after sixty hours.)

In Victorian England, giving a bouquet took on a special meaning. Tussie-mussies were small bouquets, or nosegays, put together with a variety of fragrant flowers and herbs. Each flower had a meaning and a special message, and roses were among the most popular flowers to send. If it was in full bloom, a rose meant secrecy. The color was also significant. White stood for purity, pink for love, and red for what else than passion?

But rose petals and rose hips are also welcome in the kitchen. The hips have a cranberrylike quality and can be used to make jellies and soups and as a flavoring in quick breads and muffins. The petals are used in many cuisines to decorate or flavor desserts and condiments.

Dried rose buds and petals add color as well as fragrance to potpourris, sachets, and dried herbal arrangements. The modern hybrids will provide only color, not scent, and many turn sour, but hybrid damask and Provence roses, as well as rugosas, are rich in scent. And what could be better at the end of the day than a soothing bath fragrant with the aroma of rose petals?

ROSEMARY

Rosmarinus officinalis

The Greeks and Romans believed rosemary had the power to strengthen memory, so it became a symbol of remembrance and friendship. As a sign of fidelity, it was woven into crowns worn by couples at their wedding ceremony. It was placed in the hands of the dead before burial and scattered on their graves as a sign they would not be forgotten, a custom still carried out in parts of Wales.

Rosemary has always been a religious herb, used as incense and as a safeguard from evil. A Christian fable tells how its tiny flowers turned from white to blue. To avoid Herod's soldiers, Joseph and the Virgin Mary fled with the baby Jesus to Egypt. On the way, they stopped to rest by a rosemary bush, where Mary dropped her heavy cloak. When she was rested, Mary picked up her wrap to continue the journey, and in memory of her visit, the delicate flower clusters turned blue.

TASTE: Highly aromatic, almost like incense. It tastes the way it smells and has a brothlike quality with bitter undertones. It's often combined with other herbs.

SPECIAL PROPERTIES: An excellent stimulant and all-around digestive tonic, rosemary tea is also a comforting brew when you feel a cold or the flu coming on or are bothered by a headache. Used in a bath or compress, it soothes sore muscles.

PARTS USED FOR TEA: The leaves and the flowers.

BREWING METHOD: Infusion. Use $\frac{1}{2}$ to 1 teaspoon of fresh or dried leaves, 1 teaspoon of dried flowers, or 3 teaspoons of

WHO'S THAT IN THE MOONLIGHT?

According to an old custom in

Northamptonshire, England,

if a young woman can pick twelve

sage leaves without injuring the plant at the stroke of

midnight on Christmas Eve,

she'll see the shadow of her future husband in the moonlight.

fresh flowers, in 1 cup (8 ounces) of freshly boiling water. Steep to taste and add lemon and honey.

HOW TO GROW AND HARVEST: A tender perennial, rosemary grows between three and six feet tall and likes well-drained, alkaline soil. A Mediterranean native, it grows both in full and partial sun. The highly aromatic, needlelike leaves are often gray-green and reminiscent of a fir tree's needles. The tiny flowers are white to pale blue in color and are formed on the stems at the leaf axils.

Even though rosemary is a perennial and looks tough, it's fragile when it comes to cold weather. As the temperature starts dipping close to freezing, I bring my pots indoors. Rosemary is one of those herbs you can pluck anytime, especially the new top growth along each stem. Some gardeners like to sculpt their rosemary plants. As you clip, you can sip your rosemary tea or save your sprigs for future use.

OTHER USES: What's a roast leg of lamb without rosemary? Fresh or dried, rosemary is a delicious and memorable culinary herb. In England, rosemary flowers are pounded into granulated sugar and left for several days to impart a spicy sweetness that complements fruit desserts and custards. A popular herb in aro-matherapy, rosemary is still believed to improve memory.

Next time your muscles are tired from a long or heavy workout, try warming a towel or compress with a strong solution of rosemary tea. Apply it to the sore area and feel how it comforts and eases the pain. Or, try an herbal bath. A lukewarm rosemary infusion used as a hair rinse will fight dandruff.

Rosemary is also used as a fragrance in perfume, soaps, and deodorants. Like mint, its scent repels insects.

SAGE

Salvia officinalis

As a medicinal herb, sage is a prize. Its Latin name, *salvia,* means "to be saved," and through the Middle Ages sage was believed to be a panacea for all the discomforts of mankind. The great ancient Greek physician Hippocrates believed its volatile oils helped cure illnesses of the brain and stomach.

TASTE: Common garden sage, *S. officinalis*, has a highly aromatic and characteristic taste that goes well with lemon. The leaves of fresh pineapple sage (*S. rutilans*), with their tropical fragrance, make a tea that's lovely to smell, although the flavor is weak. Another delicious tea variety is honeydew melon sage

(*S. elegans*) with its strong, fruity aroma.

SPECIAL PROPERTIES: Drinking or gargling with some warm sage tea is a classic remedy for a sore throat, canker sores, or tonsillitis. Sage tea also relieves digestion and colic.

PARTS USED FOR TEA: The leaves.

BREWING METHOD: Infusion. Use 2 teaspoons of fresh leaves, or 1 teaspoon dried, in 1 cup (8 ounces) of freshly boiling water. Steep 5 to 10 minutes, or to taste.

HOW TO GROW AND HARVEST: This hardy, perennial shrub grows up to three feet in height. There are over a hundred varieties. Depending on which you choose, the oblong leaves, placed in pairs along the stem, range from gray-green to purple in color. Sage likes a sunny spot and will grow in ordinary soil, but prefers it to be on the sandy side. It grows well from seeds or by dividing old plants and is easily brought indoors and grown in a pot.

The leaves should be harvested just before the flowers begin to bloom. They dry well when hung in small bunches.

OTHER USES: Sage is a popular culinary herb. Its distinctive flavor makes it easy to recognize in stuffings, salads, and stews. Pineapple sage gives a tropical touch to chicken recipes.

As an accent foliage, sage is often included in bouquets and wreaths because of its unusual colors.

SCENTED GERANIUM

Pelargonium x fragrans

A native of South Africa's Cape of Good Hope, scented geraniums found their way to Europe in the seventeenth century when Dutch and English sailors brought them home as mementos.

Scented geraniums (or pelargoniums) are distantly related to those geraniums whose cheery red and white flowers greet you in window boxes and sidewalk cafés. There are hundreds of species and the leaves come in all shapes, sizes, and fragrances. It's no wonder that horticultural president Thomas Jefferson included species of the fragrant plant whenever he planted a garden.

TASTE: The aroma will be characteristic of the variety used, with fragrances ranging from apple to rose, lemon, lime, nutmeg, licorice, and almond.

SPECIAL PROPERTIES: Although it is not recognized by many herbalists as a medicinal herb, scented geranium leaves possess astringent qualities, and one species, *P. antidysentericum*, has been found helpful in cases of dysentery.

PARTS USED FOR TEA: The leaves.

BREWING METHOD: Infusion. Use 2 teaspoons of fresh leaves, or 1 teaspoon dried, in 1 cup (8 ounces) of freshly boiling water. Steep 5 to 10 minutes, or to taste. Since the flavor is extremely delicate, you may wish to make a stronger cup. Rose-scented geranium combines well with mint. Other varieties are often used in herbal blends.

HOW TO GROW AND HARVEST: Usually available in nurseries, this is one plant I'm always on the lookout for in friends' gardens because it's an easy plant to propagate from cuttings. (Whenever I make scented-leaf bouquet—which lasts for weeks—I often find the stems have rooted in water.)

They are tender perennials, and many gardeners grow them as annuals and purchase new plants every year. You may shelter the plants from freezing weather by bringing pots indoors. Plants reach two feet in height, but there are also hanging varieties. Although they do fairly well in partial shade, scented geraniums like a sunny spot with well-drained soil. They add texture and variety to any garden setting, and there's nothing quite as pleasant as brushing across their leaves. Their clusters of tiny, orchidlike flowers range in color from white to lavender, but since the flowers aren't fragrant, they are often overshadowed by the showy leaves.

This collection of scented geraniums with their unusual foliage will make any patio or garden a fragrant and visual delight: *Pelargonium capitatum* (rose-scented), *P. crispum* (lemon-scented), *P. fragrans* (nutmeg-scented), *P. graveolens* 'Rober's Lemon Rose', *P. graveolens* 'Variegated Mint-scented Rose', *P. grossularioides* (coconut-scented), *P. limoneum* (lemon-scented), *P. nervosum* (lime-scented), *P. odoratissimum* 'Apple', *P. odoratissimum* 'Prince of Orange', *P. torento* 'Ginger'.

For the most aromatic tea, gather the leaves before the plant flowers. The leaves dry well when placed in baskets or on trays.

OTHER USES: Their fragrant leaves make them popular in sachets, potpourris, and herb pillows. They can also be used as an edible garnish or a mild flavoring in desserts and salads.

In Victorian England, the leaves were used as a flavoring in afternoon tea cakes. You can easily re-create this delicious tradition by using a favorite sponge cake recipe or yellow cake mix. The popular method was to line the cake pan with fresh leaves before the batter was added. (The leaves were removed after the cake had baked and cooled.) I find mincing the leaves and folding them into the batter works just as well. I also like to make a powdered sugar glaze by mixing powdered sugar with milk infused with the scented leaves.

S W E E T   C I C E L Y

Myrrhis odorata

Today, sweet cicely is often overlooked, but it's one of my favorite tea herbs. Not only does it add beauty and texture to a garden, but it makes a lovely, delicate, anise-flavored tea. Appropriately, its Latin name, *Myrrhis odorata,* is derived from the Greek word for perfume.

TASTE: A pleasant, delicate, anise flavor.

SPECIAL PROPERTIES: Gentle to the stomach, the tea helps with digestion, soothes coughs, and eases intestinal gas.

PARTS USED FOR TEA: The leaves and the seeds. The root is also used in decoction for medicinal purposes.

BREWING METHOD: Infusion. Use 2 teaspoons of fresh leaves in 1 cup (8 ounces) of freshly boiling water. The seeds can be crushed by mortar and pestle and then made into an infusion using 1 teaspoon for each cup of boiling water. In either case, steep 5 to 10 minutes, or to taste.

HOW TO GROW AND HARVEST: Sweet cicely loves a shady garden with moist, loamy soil, and will reach between two and three feet in height. Its anise-scented leaves resemble fern fronds. The thick root can be used like fennel in cooking. Although sweet cicely will grow from seeds, especially if they're self-sown from a parent plant, I find it easiest to start with a purchased seedling.

The leaves can be harvested throughout the growing season. The seed pods should be gathered while still green and hung upside down in a paper bag to collect the seeds as the pods dry and open. (Give the bag a shake or two.) The roots are harvested in the late autumn or early spring while the plant is dormant. Also, as a caution, it's not a good idea to harvest sweet cicely in the wild, since it resembles the very poisonous swamp hemlock.

OTHER USES: All parts of this plant are useful in the kitchen. Its roots can be grated like ginger and used as a flavoring in cakes and muffins. The seeds give a delicate anise flavoring that can be used as a substitute for poppy or caraway seeds. As a gathered green in salads or an edible garnish, the fernlike leaves will delight adventurous guests. Sweet cicely's volatile oils are also used to scent cosmetics and perfumes.

THYME

Thymus vulgaris; T. x citriodorus,
lemon thyme

To the Greeks, thyme stood for courage. In the Middle Ages, it was a symbol of chivalry. During the French Revolution, it signified the Republican spirit.

Thyme's fragrant sprigs have been used since ancient Greece to freshen a house and chase away insects. Today, its dried flowers are used in linen sachets to discourage pests, and a strong infusion of thyme makes a safe and fragrant disinfectant for any household surface.

TASTE: Pungent and slightly bitter, this tea is best enjoyed with honey. I prefer lemon thyme for tea because of its citrusy undertones. Rosemary is often added to thyme tea to give it more depth.

SPECIAL PROPERTIES: A warm thyme tea is soothing to sore throats and coughs as a beverage or a gargle. It relieves a stomachache or irritable bowel and is often prescribed as a gentle tonic for childhood diarrhea.

PARTS USED FOR TEA: The leaves and the flowering tops.

BREWING METHOD: Infusion. Use 3 teaspoons of fresh herb, or up to 2 teaspoons of dried, in 1 cup (8 ounces) of freshly boiling water. Steep up to 10 minutes, or to taste.

HOW TO GROW AND HARVEST: This small, shrubby perennial is a Mediterranean native that prefers dry soil and full sun. Its tiny, gray-green leaves are oval shaped and appear opposite each other on the many-branched stems. Small clusters of lilac to pink flowers appear at the end of the stems.

For the beginning gardener, thyme is an easy herb to grow. It doesn't require much maintenance and can be divided easily by separating a mature plant into several smaller ones.

The leaves can be harvested before and after flowering. The flower heads should be snipped from their stems as they begin to open. Gathered stems dry easily in bunches, and they also freeze well.

OTHER USES: Today, thyme is used primarily as a culinary herb. It's popular in many cuisines and makes a fine addition to a *bouquet garni*. Although garden thyme is most often used, lemon thyme gives an added zest to flavored vinegars, soups, and stews. Thyme-flavored honey has been a delicacy since Virgil's time and can usually been found in Greek delicatessens.

An infusion of thyme in warm bath water is soothing and refreshing, and thyme's volatile oils are often added to aftershave lotions and soaps.

WINTERGREEN

Gaultheria procumbens

Also known as teaberry, wintergreen is indigenous to North America. Its leaves were enjoyed as a natural chewing gum by Native Americans, who also brewed wintergreen tea to cure sore throats and fever. During the American Revolution, patriots sipped wintergreen as well as other "liberty" herbal teas to protest the heavy tax on English brews.

TASTE: Refreshing, with a sharp, cool aftertaste.

SPECIAL PROPERTIES: Wintergreen contains methyl salicylate, the chemical basis for aspirin, and that's why it's often brewed as a tea to reduce the pain of muscle aches and headaches. It's also a mild diuretic.

PARTS USED FOR TEA: The leaves.

BREWING METHOD: Infusion. Use 2 teaspoons of fresh leaves, or 1 heaping teaspoon dried, in 1 cup (8 ounces) of freshly boiling water. Steep for 5 to 10 minutes, or to taste.

HOW TO GROW AND HARVEST: An attractive ground cover, this perennial has shiny, elliptical leaves and spreads by creeping underground stems that send up erect branches. The white, bell-shaped flowers turn to scarlet berries in the fall.

Wintergreen likes shade. In the wild, it's often found growing under rhododendrons and pine trees. It can grow from seeds or cuttings. I'll often dig up lengths of the underground stem and replant them directly in moist soil. (However, my experience is that transplanting wild plants is not as successful as purchasing ones that are grown commercially.)

Leaves can be gathered anytime, although the tender leaves taste best before the flowers bloom.

OTHER USES: An essential component of toothpastes, cough drops, and healing creams for tired muscles, wintergreen is used as a flavoring and analgesic ingredient in many over-the-counter drugs. Unless your skin is sensitive to wintergreen's volatile oil, another relaxing home remedy after working out is a soothing herbal bath made with a wintergreen infusion.

Other Herbal Tea Plants

ANISE HYSSOP (*Agastache foeniculum*) is one of my favorite anise-scented herbs. It's somewhat difficult to find, but if you do, buy it. The fresh leaves will give you a delightful beverage. To make a cup, use 2 teaspoons of the fresh herb, or ½ to 1 teaspoon of the dried herb, in 1 cup (8 ounces) of freshly boiling water. Steep for 5 to 10 minutes, or to taste.

GINSENG (*Panax quinquefolium,* American ginseng; *P. ginseng,* Korean or Chinese ginseng) has been known as a wonder drug for centuries. First used in China, ginseng has been heralded as an aphrodisiac, a key to longevity, and a cure-all of many human ailments. Ginseng's root often resembles the human form, and its alleged powers may partly stem from earlier beliefs that a plant's shape echoed its curative powers. There are many commercial ginseng teas on the market, and you can find them as well as the dried roots in health food stores and Asian grocery stores. To make a decoction, use ½ teaspoon of the powdered root to each cup (8 ounces) of boiling water, then simmer for 10 minutes.

HIBISCUS (*Hibiscus abelmoschus, H. sabdariffa*), a native of Africa, is related to the bushy, ornamental shrub that decorates many tropical gardens and whose flower was a favorite Carmen Miranda accessory. The calyces, which form the outer protective covering of the flower buds, are dried and used to make a rosy, citrus-flavored tea. (In recipes, the calyces are referred to as hibiscus flowers.) Hibiscus is a very popular addition to many commercial herbal tea blends, and one you'll have fun experimenting with. To make an infusion, use 2 teaspoons or more of the dried hibiscus flowers in 1 cup (8 ounces) of freshly boiling water. Steep for 5 to 10 minutes or to taste. (See Agua de Jamaica recipe on page 48.)

Unless you live in the tropics where this plant grows naturally, it's best to buy the dried calyces from health- and natural-food stores. Hibiscus is also available from herbal tea sources. (See Mail Order Sources, page 104.)

HOPS (*Humulus lupulus*) are those small, cone-like flowers (strobiles) that flavor and preserve beer. They are also used to brew a home remedy that works as a mild sedative, relieving stress and tension and helping you get a good night's sleep. The mellow tea has a peppery, bitter taste. To make an infusion, use 2 teaspoons of fresh or freeze-dried hops, in 1 cup (8 ounces) of freshly boiling water. Steep for 5 minutes.

HOREHOUND (*Marrubium vulgare)* makes a bittersweet tea with musky undertones that has soothed sore throats and coughing spells since Roman times. Candied horehound still makes a popular hard candy cough drop to suck during a movie or concert when you don't want to make a peep.

To make an infusion, use 2 teaspoons of fresh leaves, or ½ to 1 teaspoon of the dried leaves, in 1 cup (8 ounces) of freshly boiling water. Steep for 10 minutes.

LEMON GRASS (*Cymbopogon citratus*) is relatively new to the herbal tea market and it brings a citrus note to many blends. The fresh or dried blades have a perfumy lemon flavor that is a staple of Thai and Vietnamese cuisine. (The herb contains the same essential oil that's in lemon peel.) Lemon grass is available fresh or dried in Asian markets,

and I've ordered the dried blades through herbal suppliers. (See Herbal Teas for Healing and Pleasure, page 100.)

To make an infusion, use 2 teaspoons of fresh blades, or 1 heaping teaspoon of dried, in 1 cup (8 ounces) of freshly boiling water. Steep for 5 to 10 minutes, or to taste.

LEMON VERBENA (*Aloysia triphylla*) makes a delightful lemon-lime tea that aids digestion and helps put you to sleep. To make an infusion, use 2 teaspoons of the fresh leaves, or 1 heaping teaspoon of the dried leaves, in 1 cup (8 ounces) of freshly boiling water. Steep for 5 to 10 minutes, or to taste.

Lemon verbena is easy to grow. Its fragrant foliage is attractive in a backyard or container garden and makes a lovely accent to floral bouquets, especially tussie-mussies. Scarlett O'Hara's favorite scent, lemon verbena is also used in potpourris and as a fresh ingredient and garnish in culinary dishes.

LINDEN FLOWERS (*Tilia europaea* and other species) have a taste that's similar to chamomile and they make an excellent aromatic tea, but because they're expensive to harvest, they don't often show up in

North American tea blends. A strong medicinal infusion is believed to help relax blood vessels and prevent arteriosclerosis. Dried linden flowers can be found in herbal tea shops, and they're worth the hunt, especially when you blend them with peppermint tea. To make an infusion, use 1 teaspoon of the dried blossoms in 1 cup (8 ounces) of freshly boiling water. Steep for 5 minutes.

RED CLOVER (*Trifolium pratense*) is to many just a roadside plant that scatters itself in meadows and vacant lots, but its red to purple blossoms make a delicately scented tea that combines well with mint, lemon balm, and dried rose hips. It is used as a remedy for coughs and bronchitis by making an infusion of 1 teaspoon dried clover blossoms in 1 cup (8 ounces) of freshly boiling water. Steep for 5 to 10 minutes.

SWEET WOODRUFF (*Asperula odorata*) leaves have little aroma when first gathered, but after they've dried they release the lovely scents of vanilla and fresh-mowed hay. In Germany, the leaves are used as a flavoring in the May wine, part of a ritual dating back to the Druids.

With its small white flowers and whorls of dark green leaves, the woodland plant makes an attractive ground covering in shady spots. I often use its sprigs in small, fresh bouquets, and I dry bunches to use like lavender between sheets and linens.

Sweet woodruff tea has been used as a home remedy for headaches and as a digestive tonic since the Middle Ages, but recent FDA research suggests it's toxic in large quantities and should only be used only for flavoring alcoholic beverages like May wine.

VALERIAN (*Valeriana officinalis*) is nature's tranquilizer. During the First and Second World Wars, an infusion of the unpeeled and macerated root helped calm shell-shock victims. In England, it was prescribed for civilians trying to cope with the anxiety of constant air raids. Taken in small doses, valerian relieves pain and promotes sleep, but constant use may cause headaches. Its unpleasant taste is often disguised with mint. Valerian closely parallels the effects of catnip, right down to its feline appeal.

To make a decoction, use 1 heaping teaspoon of the cut, dried root in to each cup (8 ounces) of boiling water. Simmer for 15 to 20 minutes.

Spices for Tea

We think of spices as highly aromatic seasonings to flavor food and give it zest. But the difference between an herb and a spice is not always clear, especially when making an herbal tea. Herbs tend to be more delicate and subtle in flavor and usually come from the leafy parts of the plant, while spices, known for their dramatic and exotic flavors, are harvested from the bark, roots, seeds, flowers, and fruits. When making tea from a spice, decoction is usually the method used because the volatile oils are more difficult to release. (See Preparing Your Own Cup, page 31.)

CARDAMOM (*Elettaria cardamomum*) seeds have a gentle, peppery, gingery flavor used in curry powders and as a flavoring in cakes and baked goods. In beverages, cardamom flavors tea and coffee. Cardamom tea will relieve indigestion and help to stimulate an appetite. (The seeds are also quite tasty on their own.) The seeds stay fresh longer if you keep them in their pods until you decide to use them. Cardamom pods are easily found in the spice section of your supermarket.

To make an infusion, use 1 heaping teaspoon of the freshly crushed seeds in 1 cup (8 ounces) of freshly boiling water. Steep for 5 to 10 minutes, or to taste.

CINNAMON (*Cinnamomum zeylanicum*) has a sweet, aromatic flavor that makes us think of warm cookies and mulled wine. In ancient times, it was used to embalm Egyptian royalty and to create love potions for wealthy Romans. Cinnamon comes from the dried inner bark of a fast-growing tropical tree that is native to Sri Lanka and India. Medicinally, cinnamon aids in digestion and helps with nausea and gas. As a culinary spice, it's international, flavoring sweet and savory dishes in a multitude of cuisines. What's fall without the taste of cinnamon in apple pie? What's winter without the aroma of cinnamon in herbal wreaths and steaming cider?

When you want the aromatic zest of cinnamon in your tea, add a small pinch of the powder, to taste, when brewing. Use stick cinnamon when mulling beverages or when you want a handy stir stick.

CLOVES (*Syzygium aromaticum*) are the dried, unopened flower buds of a tropical tree native to the Moluccas, once known as the Spice Islands. Their sharp, distinctive taste is familiar to anyone who has opened a kitchen spice cabinet. Cloves are often used to flavor teas, coffees, and mulled beverages.

When flavoring herbal teas, add a few cloves to your freshly boiling water and infuse with your herb of choice.

GINGER (*Zingiber officinale*) root has been pleasing palates since the ancient Greeks first made gingerbread from the ginger root, which is actually a rhizome or underground stem. Peppery and slightly sweet in taste, with a pungent and spicy aroma, ginger tea has been used for centuries to soothe indigestion and warm a chill. Fresh ginger makes a delicious flavoring in many herbal teas and is easy to find in most supermarkets.

One of my favorite morning teas is made by simply grating 2 teaspoons of the fresh, unpeeled root and adding it to a 2-cup mint leaf infusion. After steeping, enjoy it right away because ginger's potent flavor continues to increase even after it's strained. For a sweet and unusual alternative to sugar, try crystallized ginger. Both fresh and crystallized ginger are available at the supermarket. The dried root is found in health food stores and herbal shops.

NUTMEG (*Myristica fragrans*) comes from the fruit kernel of a tree grown in the Moluccas. (The outside covering of the nutmeg kernel is made into mace.) As a medicinal spice, a decoction of nutmeg is used to treat chronic colitis and indigestion. Grated nutmeg adds a warm, aromatic taste to tea, coffee, and mulled beverages. To flavor tea, add a sprinkling of grated nutmeg to the freshly boiling water along with your herb of choice.

Herbal Teas for Healing and Pleasure

HERBAL TEAS FOR HEALTH AND HEALING

Many herbal teas are brewed as home remedies for common ailments. I've listed the herbs described in this book as potential aids for certain complaints, but I caution you not to self-treat any serious illness. If you are sick, see your doctor.

To make herbal teas listed below, look in the Your Guide To Herbs chapter for the specific herb and its brewing method. Remember, when professional herbalists prescribe infusions for their clients, the concentrations are more potent and are usually taken several times a day.

You may also want to try combining some of the herbs listed below and blending their medicinal powers as well as their flavors. And, if you like your beverage sweetened, try honey. It's soothing and will help control coughing naturally.

TO RELIEVE NASAL CONGESTION BY STEAM INHALATION: Chamomile, Lemon balm, Mint. Make double the amount of your standard infusion and place it in a bowl. Or, place 2 to 3 tablespoons of the dried herb in the bowl and pour boiling water over it. Drape a towel over your head and the basin to keep the steam from escaping. Breathe as you normally would for up to 10 minutes. Repeat when necessary.

TO RELIEVE COLDS AND FLU: Angelica, Borage, Catnip, Chamomile, Lemon balm, Rose, Rosemary

TO EASE COUGHS: Angelica, Aniseed, Bergamot, Borage, Clover, Horehound, Marjoram, Sweet cicely, Thyme

TO AID DIGESTION: Angelica, Anise, Cinnamon, Fennel, Lemon balm, Lemon verbena, Mint, Oregano, Rosemary, Sage, Sweet cicely

TO RELIEVE HEADACHES: Lavender, Marjoram, Mint, Rosemary, Valerian, Wintergreen

TO RELIEVE INDIGESTION AND GAS: Calendula, Cardamom, Catnip, Chamomile, Cinnamon, Fennel, Ginger, Mint, Oregano, Parsley, Sage, Sweet cicely, Thyme

TO REDUCE NAUSEA: Basil, Bergamot, Chamomile, Cinnamon, Mint

TO LIFT THE SPIRITS: Basil, Lavender, Mint

TO RELIEVE INSOMNIA AND AID SLEEP: Anise, Catnip, Chamomile, Hops, Lemon verbena, Valerian

TO HELP RELIEVE SORE THROATS: Bergamot, Horehound, Oregano (as a gargle), Raspberry Leaf (as a gargle), Rose, Sage (as a gargle), Thyme (as a gargle)

TO RELIEVE STRESS AND TENSION: Catnip, Chamomile, Lavender, Lemon balm, Mint, Valerian

TO REDUCE WATER RETENTION: Dandelion, Parsley, Raspberry, Wintergreen

HERBAL TEAS FOR BATH AND PLEASURE

It may seem strange to include a list of bath herbs in a book on herbal tea, but many of the same infusions you brew to enjoy as a beverage will transform your bath into an invigorating, refreshing, or soothing beauty treatment. It all depends on the herbal infusion you choose.

The easiest way to add herbs to your bath is to make a concentrated infusion, using $\frac{1}{2}$ cup of the dried herbs to 3 cups of boiling water. Let the infusion steep for 15 to 20 minutes, then strain and add the warmed brew to your bath water. Other options: use purchased tea bags, like mint and chamomile; purchase re-usable muslin bags with drawstrings from herbal suppliers; or make your own muslin tea bags. (See Creating Your Own Blends, page 43.)

Next time you're brewing a morning cup of herbal tea, make some extra and save it for your evening bath. While it may not be as potent—unless you make close to a quart—it will certainly give rise to some lovely aromas.

The one thing you want to avoid is tossing the loose herbs into the water. Besides sticking all over your body, they can wreak havoc on a drain.

FOR AROMATIC BATHS: Lavender, Lemon balm, Lemon verbena, Mint, Rose flowers, Rosemary, Scented geraniums

FOR SOOTHING BATHS: Catnip, Chamomile, Hops, Lemon balm, Linden flowers, Marjoram, Rose, Rosemary, Thyme, Valerian, Wintergreen

FOR STIMULATING BATHS: Basil, Calendula, Fennel, Lavender, Marjoram, Mint, Rosemary, Sage, Thyme

Mail Order Sources

The most immediate source for seeds, plants, and garden supplies is your local nursery or garden center, so enjoy getting to know them. Besides being very helpful in answering specific plant questions and explaining growing conditions, they're often able to help you locate difficult-to-find herbs. Many of the suppliers listed below also carry herbal tea supplies, such as bags and infusers, and dried herbs you're not able to grow.

W. Atlee Burpee and Company
300 Park Avenue
Warminster, PA 18974
(215) 674-4900
seeds, plants, gardening supplies
catalog free

Companion Plants
7247 N. Coolville Ridge Road
Athens, OH 45701
(614) 592-4643
common and exotic herb seeds and plants from around the world
catalog $3

Cook's Garden
P.O. Box 535
Londonderry, VT 05148
(802) 824-3400; fax (802) 824-3027
organically grown seeds and supplies for the kitchen garden
catalog free

Goodwin Creek Gardens
P.O. Box 83
Williams, OR 97544

(541) 846-7357
Native American herbs, medicinals, lavenders,
and hummingbird/butterfly plants
catalog $1

The Herbfarm
32804 Issaquah–Fall City Road
Fall City, WA 98024
(206) 784-2222
herbfax (206) 222-7004 (great information
line for people with fax machines)
seeds and plants, garden, kitchen, and craft
supplies, and publications
catalog free

Herbally Yours
P.O. Box 26
Changewater, NJ 07831
(908) 689-6140
dried herbs, medicinal herbs, spices, tea, and
herbal and kitchen supplies
catalog $1

Logee's Greenhouses
141 North Street
Danielson, CT 06239
(203) 774-8038
a collection of rare plants and a variety of herbs
catalog $3, deductible with your order

Meadowbrook Herb Garden
Route 138
Wyoming, RI 02898
(401) 539-7603
seeds, medicinal and beverage teas, and culinary
herbs and spices
pamphlet free

Mom's Head Gardens
4153 Langer Avenue
Santa Rosa, CA 95407
(707) 585-8575
organically grown medicinal and culinary
herbs, herbal workshops
catalog $1.25

Nichols Garden Catalog
1190 North Pacific Highway
Albany, OR 97321-4580
(503) 928-9280
seeds and plants, garden tools, teas, essential
oils, and books
catalog free

Premier Botanicals Ltd.
8801 Buena Vista Road
Albany, OR 97321
(541) 926-5945; fax (541) 928-2730
essential oils, dried herbs, specializing in
lavender
catalog free

Rasland Farm
Route 1, Box 65C
Goodwin, NC 28344
(910) 567-2705
seeds and plants, craft supplies, herbal products, and publications
catalog $2.50

Richters Herbs
357 Highway 47
Goodwood, Ontario
L0C 1A0 Canada
(905) 640-6677
E-mail: catalogue@richters.com
seeds and plants, gardening, medicinal and herbal supplies, and publications
catalog free

Sandy Mush Herb Nursery
316 Surrett Cove Road
Leicester, NC 28748-9622
(704) 683-2014
broad selection of seeds and plants and valuable information
detailed handbook / catalog $4,
free plant list

Sunburst Bottle Company
5710 Auburn Boulevard, #7
Sacramento, CA 95841
(916) 348-5576
clear and cobalt blue bottles and vials
catalog $2

Tinmouth Channel Farm
Herbs, Naturally
Box 428B-HCD
Tinmouth, VT 05773
(802) 446-2812
herb seeds and Vermont certified organic herb plants
catalog $2

Well-Sweep Herb Farm
205 Mt. Bethel Road
Port Murray, NJ 07865
(908) 852-5390
broad selection of seeds, plants, herbal supplies, gifts, and books
detailed catalog $2

Bibliography

With the growing interest in herbs for every season of our lives, many more books and magazines are devoted to the subject. You can find a rich source of good information in your library and local bookstores. Other places to browse are your garden center, supermarket, and herb shops. The following list of books and magazines are ones I've enjoyed and found entertaining as well as knowledgeable.

BOOKS

Blose, Nora, and Dawn Cusick. *Herb Drying Handbook.* New York: Sterling Publications, 1993.

Boxer, Arabella, and Philippa Back. *The Herb Book.* London: Octopus Books, 1980.

Bremness, Lesley. *World of Herbs.* New York: Crescent Books, 1990.

D'Andrea, Jeanne. *Ancient Herbs in the J. Paul Getty Museum Gardens.* Malibu, CA: The J. Paul Getty Museum, 1989.

Grieve, Mrs. M. *A Modern Herbal.* 2 vols. New York: Dover Publications, 1971.

Grieve, Mrs. M. *Culinary Herbs and Condiments.* New York: Harcourt, Brace and Company, 1934.

Hoffmann, David. *The New Holistic Herbal.* New York: Barnes & Noble, 1990.

Marcin, Marietta Marshall. *The Herbal Tea Garden.* Pownal, VT: Storey Communications, 1993.

Ody, Penelope. *The Complete Medicinal Herbal.* London: Dorling Kindersley, 1993.

Ody, Penelope. *Home Herbal.* London: Dorling Kindersley, 1995.

Reid, Shirley. *A Practical Step-by-Step Guide to Herbs for the Home and Garden.* Australia: Cornstalk Publishing, a division of HarperCollins, 1991.

The Republic of Tea. *The Book of Tea & Herbs.* Santa Rosa, CA: The Cole Group, 1993.

Rodale's Illustrated Encyclopedia of Herbs. Emmaus, PA: Rodale Press, 1987.

Simon & Schuster's Guide to Herbs and Spices. New York: A Fireside Book, Simon & Schuster, 1990.

Stevenson, Violet. *A Modern Herbal.* New York: Crescent Books, Crown Publishers, 1974.

Stewart, Hilary. *Wild Teas, Coffees & Cordials.* Seattle, WA: University of Washington Press, 1981.

Stuckey, Maggie. *The Complete Herb Book.* New York: Berkley Books, 1994.

Shafer, Violet. *Herbcraft: A Compendium of Myths, Romance and Commonsense.* San Francisco: Yerba Buena Press, 1971.

Simmons, Adelma Grenier. *Herb Gardening in Five Seasons.* New York: Plume, Penguin Books, 1990.

Tyler, Varro. *Herbs of Choice: The Therapeutic Use of Phytomedicinals.* New York: Pharmaceutical Products Press, 1994.

MAGAZINES

The Herb Companion, Interweave Press, 201 East Fourth Street, Loveland, CO 80537 (bimonthly). Note: I have often used the ads in this publication to find supplies and herbs.

The Herb Quarterly, P.O. Box 689, San Anselmo, CA 94960 (quarterly).

Index

Ginger, 51, 99, 101
Ginseng, 94

H

Healing teas. *See* Home remedies
Herbal teas. *See also individual herbs*
  history of, 4, 6–7
  making, 31–38
  purchasing, 14
  recipes, 47–50
  serving, 39
Herb House Winter Tea, 49
Herbs. *See also individual herbs*
  botanical names of, 26–27
  drying, 22, 24–25
  growing, 16, 18–21
  harvesting, 21–22
  history of, 4, 6–7
  purchasing, 14–15, 38
  storing, 25, 28–29
  symbolic meanings of, 55
  wildcrafting, 15–16
Hibiscus, 55, 94
Home remedies, 7–8, 10, 100–101
Honeys, herbal, 53
Hops, 55, 96, 101, 103
Horehound, 96, 101

I

Ice cubes, herbal, 41
Infusions, 10, 35, 37, 38

L

Lavender, 55, 71, 73, 101, 103
Lemon balm, 55, 73, 75, 100, 101, 103
Lemon grass, 96
Lemon verbena, 96, 101, 103
Linden flowers, 96–97, 103

M

Marjoram, 55, 75, 77, 101, 103
Milk, 39
Mint, 55, 76, 77–79, 100, 101, 103
Mint Syrup with Orange Essence, 52

N

Nutmeg, 99

O

Oregano, 79, 81, 101
Oswego tea. *See* Bergamot

P

Parsley, 55, 80, 81–82, 101
Pelargoniums. *See* Scented geraniums
Peppermint and Chai Spice Tea, 47
Pot marigold. *See* Calendula

R

Raspberry leaf, 55, 82–83, 101
Red clover, 97
Relax Herbal Tea, 49
Rose, 55, 83, 85–86, 100, 101, 103